Researching Public Records

How to Get Anything on Anybody

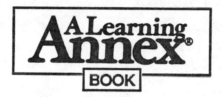

Vincent Parco

A Citadel Press Book
Published by Carol Publishing Group

Carol Publishing Group Edition - 19

Copyright © 1994 by Vincent Parco

A Citadel Press Book
Published by Carol Publishing Group
Citadel Press is a registered trademark of Carol Communications, Inc.
Editorial Offices: 600 Madison Avenue, New York, NY 10022
Sales & Distribution Offices: 120 Enterprise Avenue, Secaucus, NJ 07094
In Canada: Canadian Manda Group, P.O. Box 920, Station U, Toronto, Ontario, M8Z 5P9, Canada
Queries regarding rights and permissions should be addressed to:
Carol Publishing Group, 600 Madison Avenue, New York, NY 10022

Manufactured in the United States of America
ISBN 0-8065-1522-8

10 9 8 7 6 5 4 3 2

Carol Publishing Group books are available at special discounts for bulk purchases, sales promotions, fund raising, or educational purposes. Special editions can also be created to specifications. For details contact: Special Sales Department, Carol Publishing Group, 120 Enterprise Ave., Secaucus, NJ 07094

Library of Congress Cataloging-in-Publication Data

Parco, Vincent
   Researching public records: how to get anything on anybody/ by Vincent Parco.
         p.   cm.
   "A Learning Annex book."
1. Public records—United States—States—Handbooks, manuals, etc.
2. Biography—Research—Methodology—Handbooks, manuals, etc.
3. Investigations—Handbooks, manuals, etc. I. Title.
JK2445.P82P37   1994
027.5'0973—dc20   93-44224
                                          CIP

Contents

PART II: *Kinds of Searches*

PART III: *Future Steps*

Acknowledgments

Special thanks to Harry Javer, director of The Learning Annex; Ted Mullany, the second best investigator I know; Nick Vasile, who puts up with me; and especially Irene Korn, whose writing and editing assistance was invaluable in completing this book.

Introduction

There are many reasons to write a book. Mine is quite simply the joy I get from sharing what I know with people who are interested.

Through the years, it has given me great joy to teach classes at The Learning Annex, specifically "Researching Public Records" and "How to Get Anything on Anybody." My students and others in my business have frequently asked if there are any good books they can read for more information. You can imagine, then, how thrilled I was when The Learning Annex asked me to put together a book based on these classes. This book is an overview of both those topics.

In the seven years that I worked for government agencies, such as the Department of State, the New York State Department of Education/Division of Professional Discipline, and the Office of Professional Medical Conduct with the New York State Health Department, I learned that public record searches were often essential either to crack a case or to facilitate closing the case.

Public records are important by the mere fact that they are easily attainable and cost little. An individual can save a lot of money by searching records and documents as opposed to hiring a private investigator or an attorney to perform these tasks instead. But public records are sometimes only the beginning. There are a variety of other techniques that professional private investigators use to obtain information, and many of them are accessible to any individual.

Information is power, whether you want to know more about a person you are romantically involved with, want to do research for an article or book, want to be better prepared for negotiating the price of a house or business, are getting ready to enter the field of private investigating, or have just about any other aim.

I have tried to keep this book very simple, easy to read, and interesting; but most of all I have filled it with information that everyone can use in their day-to-day activities. *Getting Anything on Anybody* is designed to show you how to get all sorts of information using a variety of methods. They are methods that I, as a licensed private investigator, use in the localities where I practice. Be aware that laws governing various methods of information gathering can vary from state to state, even city to city. I always work very closely with my attorney to ensure the legality of my methods in different geographical areas. You should too.

Part I
Sources of Information

1 | *Just the Facts*

Virtually everyone has something to hide. And for every person hiding something, there's usually at least one other person equally interested in finding out that information. You probably already have something specific in mind that you want to find out. It might be as straightforward as trying to locate an old college boyfriend or as potentially complicated as wanting to find out what happened to the child you gave up for adoption. Tracing your own genealogy could take you far back in time and across countless other countries.

Some cases involve people who are just confirming the information they already have, such as double-checking the background of a potential employee or business venture or collecting the evidence that a spouse really is cheating. At other times, people have good reason for wanting to obtain information that could get someone else "in trouble"— maybe they want to prove that a difficult neighbor has a record of previous bad behavior or verify that their tenant is engaging in illegal business so eviction can proceed.

Whatever your purpose, the first place to start almost any search for information is with the public records—information that's accessible to any person for any reason. By the way, the gathering and recording of this information is paid for by your tax dollars, so you don't ever have to feel guilty about exercising your right to search these records.

Part I of this book, "Sources of Information," will tell you
everything you need to know about the various kinds of
public records, including what information you can get from
which records, where to go to find the information you need,
and what to do with it once you have it. In addition to public
records, Part I includes information on other means of
gathering information, such as computer databases, surveillance, subterfuge, and—yes—digging through the trash!

Once you're familiar with the various ways of obtaining
information, Part II, "Kinds of Searches," will take you step-
by-step through the procedures for searching for various
kinds of information. Real-life examples will show you
exactly how one piece of information can lead to other
needed pieces. And, just for the record: The names *have*
been changed to protect the innocent.

Part III includes other related information, such as ways to
protect your own privacy, how to go about being a licensed
private investigator, and publications and sources for addi-
tional information.

Getting Started

Before you start any kind of investigation, there are a few
basic things you need to know. First of all, you are *always*
allowed to be your own private investigator. You don't need
anyone's permission, a license, or anything else to look up
public records and do your own research. In fact, there's
even a law—the Freedom of Information Act—that guaran-
tees your right to obtain information from federal records.
There are certain restrictions—for example, in some cases,
you'll need to show "just cause"—but for the most part, you
can obtain any information you want simply because you
want to. Some states, too, have passed their own Freedom of
Information Acts, making it easier for you to access state and
local records.

There are standard forms to fill out to obtain certain federal records; if these aren't available, you can write a letter starting with the phrase: "Pursuant to the Freedom of Information Act, I would like the following information..." When you deal with people in person, you can simply ask for the information you need without giving any justification for the search.

Although you can always do your own investigating and information gathering, in most states you can't perform these services for someone else for a fee if you don't have a license. It's also against the law to represent yourself as a licensed private investigator if you're not. (See Chapter 6 for information about hiring a private investigator and Chapter 14 for information about obtaining your own license.)

Organizing Your Search

Before you actually *do* anything, you should figure out what information you already have and what information you're looking for. Write down everything you know about the person or business in question, no matter how seemingly irrelevant. Include basic facts, such as name, address, phone number, birth date, Social Security number, age, height, weight, hair and eye color, occupation, and anything else you know. Of course, you might not know anything more than the person's name at this point, but that's OK. For now, you just want a record of what information you do have. The chapters to follow will tell you how to learn the facts you don't yet have.

The second step is to determine what kind of information you are looking for. You might not know exactly what that is at this point, but define some sort of goal. It might be as broad as finding out if your husband is cheating on you or as specific as proving that he was with Madam X from 7:00 to 9:00 P.M. on the Friday before Thanksgiving. In many cases, you really have no idea at this point what you might come across. In such situations, your goal might simply be "to find out everything possible about the background of Company X and its owners."

To begin with, your equipment needs will be basic: telephone, paper, pen, maybe some envelopes and stamps. As you proceed, you might find that you need or want to use video or audio recorders or other tools of surveillance. If you do reach that point, it's usually advisable to hire someone who really knows what the score is (not just *how* to use those tools, but when, where, and under what circumstances it's *legal* to use them).

That's all the preparation that's needed. Whenever you're ready, turn the page to begin your search. Happy hunting!

2 | *Basic Public Records*

Whether you're trying to find someone, do a background check, trace your own genealogy, or just gather general information about someone, public records that contain personal information are generally the place to start. For almost any kind of search, you will want to know—or confirm—as soon as possible the person's full name and date of birth.

Knowing just these two facts can lead you to a wealth of other information, including current address, telephone number, and other personal information. These facts are usually necessary even when you are investigating someone solely for business purposes. The following kinds of records are the ones most likely to provide you with that information. Most of them can be found in a local Hall of Records, County Courthouse, or offices located in the state capital.

Board of Elections

If you know—or can guess—the county and state in which the person lives, the records from the Board of Elections, in some states called the Registrar of Voters, are a natural starting point. What can you find out from these records?

1. Confirmation that a person lives in a certain
county and state.

2. Verification of full name.
3. Exact date of birth. Certain public records can only be obtained if you have the exact date of birth, so it's one of the first things you need to establish or confirm.
4. Personal facts, such as height and color of eyes.
5. Current address and length of residence there.
6. Previous address if the person lived at a different address the last time they voted in an election in that state.
7. Telephone number: Voters are not required to provide their telephone number if it's not listed, but many do anyway. This can be a very easy, legal way to find an unpublished telephone number.
8. Immigration status, if applicable.
9. Enrollment in a political party.

(Bear in mind that you won't find records for everyone with the Board of Elections. You'll only find information on people who are registered to vote. If the person you are seeking information about is not of an age to vote or simply hasn't registered, you're out of luck.)

There are two ways to approach a search for registration information.

1. Start with the name of the person about whom you want information. If you don't have an exact address, chances are you will find information for more than one person with that name. Even if you don't know the exact age of the person, you can use the date of birth for each person as a method of elimination. For example, it's a pretty safe bet that the grandmotherly-looking woman you're looking for wasn't born in 1959 and the young man your daughter is dating wasn't born in 1927.

2. If you have an address, you can look up the address

of the building and see who is registered to vote from that address. Of course, just because a person lives at a certain address does not mean that they are the owner of a particular property, but it is a good way to start your search for the owner. It's also a good way to determine if the owner actually does live at a certain address, particularly if there's some question about residency. When the building in question is a multi-unit dwelling, such as an apartment building, this same kind of search is one way of ascertaining who is actually living in certain units and if those people are the ones to whom the unit is legally rented.

The Board of Elections can also supply information about politicians, including political contributions and other personal facts. School district board members, too, are listed in this office.

Department of Motor Vehicles

The name of this department varies by state, and might be listed under another name, such as the Driver's License Division or Motor Vehicle Division of some other agency, the Department of Transportation, say, or the Department of Public Safety. Whatever its name, the department is located in the capital of the state you're interested in.

In most states, driver's license information is public record, although, at present, Massachusetts and Washington will not supply this information at all, and certain states require written permission from the licensee. In most states, all you need is the person's full name and birth date to obtain the records; in some you also need the driver's license number. Check with the department in a particular state to find out its exact rules.

Since most adults these days do have a driver's license, this department is a good source of information about most people. You do, however, need to know in which state the license was obtained. If you know what state the person currently lives in, that's the most logical starting point. Other common possibilities include the state where the person was born, the state of the last known address, and the state where the original license was obtained.

The information you can receive from this department includes the following:

- Confirmation of full name and date of birth
- Height and eye color
- Driving record, including accidents, tickets, and suspensions
- Date issued and date of expiration
- Restrictions on driving

You can also do a backward kind of search through this department, starting with the license plate number or vehicle tag number, if you want to find out who owns a particular car. From these numbers, you should be able to get such information as the name and address of the person to whom the vehicle is registered, the vehicle's identification numbers, the name of the owner's insurance company, date of registration and expiration, lien holder, and the year, model, and color of the vehicle.

One huge caveat here: The person you saw in a particular vehicle might not be the person to whom the vehicle is registered. In other words, you might end up with a wealth of information about the wrong person.

A couple of other things to be aware of: If you are trying to do research on a police officer, judge, or other government official, you might well get their work address instead of their home address (this is a method of protection). If you find out a vehicle is registered to a company rather than an individual, an officer of that company will be named on the registration.

The National Driver's Registration Service is an agency established to help law enforcement officials and insurance companies trace people with a suspended or revoked license in one state who apply for a license in another state. Contact it at the U.S. Department of Commerce, 1717 H Street, Washington, D.C. 20510 for more information.

The United States Post Office

If you have a recent old address for a person and are looking for their new address, the Post Office is the place for you. It will give you the person's forwarding address if the individual has moved within the past year. There's a small fee for this service and also a flip side to it: For the same small fee, any individual can request that this information *not* be made available to other people. The good thing is that most people aren't aware that's an option.

If you have the luxury of time, another way to obtain a forwarding address is to write to the individual at the old address. Clearly write on the envelope: "Do not forward. Address correction requested." In such a case, if there is a forwarding address, your original letter will be returned to you with the person's new address.

You can also find out from the Post Office the name and address of any particular Post Office (P. O.) Box holder if the box holder is a business. However, without a court order, the Post Office will not disclose information about *individuals* who hold boxes. In addition, you can find out from the Post Office the names of all individuals receiving mail at any given address. If you have a zip code, but aren't sure what city or part of city the code is for, the Post Office can tell you.

The Bureau of Vital Statistics

Also frequently called the Department of Vital

Certificates and other similar names, this is the state office—located in the state capital—that catalogs and files what is referred to as *vital records:* birth, death, and marriage records. These records are also maintained by county vital statistics offices, and oftentimes religious institutions maintain similar records.

Birth Records

In a typical "Catch-22" situation, birth records are public information and available to everyone except those who usually want them most—adoptees. From a typical birth certificate, you can find out the date, time, and place of birth, as well as the name of the parents and the sex and name of the baby. These records are generally useful for any kind of genealogical search, background search, or confirmation that a person is who he or she claims to be.

In the case of adoptions, the original birth certificate is sealed by the court on the day the adoption is final and can only thereafter be opened by court order. Adoptees then receive an *amended birth certificate,* which does not have any identifying information, such as the names of the natural parents or place of birth. For more information on adoptees' birth certificates, see Chapter 8, "Adoptee/Birth Parent Searches."

Death Records

The most important information you can obtain from death records is confirmation that an individual truly is dead. The typical death certificate is prepared by either the attending physician, funeral director, hospital authority, or coroner. Death records will generally contain the person's age, birth name, date and place of birth, last known address, physical description, cause of death, results of autopsy, names of next of kin, funeral director, cemetery interred or crematory, as well as the person's occupation or military record.

Death records are worth checking if you are looking for someone you suspect is no longer living and in certain instances where you believe a person is falsely using the name of someone deceased.

While a death record will prove that someone is dead, the lack of a death record will not prove that someone is *not* dead. Thousands of people who die each year are never identified; examples range from a simple natural death away from home when the person is not carrying identification to the more macabre instances of murder.

Another way to ascertain death is through the Social Security Administration, which is usually one of the first offices notified of a death.

For information on citizens who have died outside of the United States, write to Passport Services, Correspondence Branch, U.S. Department of State, Washington, D.C. 20524. Deaths outside the United States are generally reported to the U.S. consular office, which then fills out a Report of the Death of American Citizen Abroad. A copy is then filed permanently in the U.S. Department of State.

In case of death of members of the armed forces outside of the United States, a report is made to the branch the person served in at the time of decease. For the Army, Navy, Marines, or Air Force, write to the Secretary of Defense, Washington, D.C. 20301; for the Coast Guard, write Commandant, P. S., U.S. Coast Guard, Washington, D.C. 20226.

Marriage Records

As in the case of death records, marriage records can prove that a marriage took place, but the lack of records will not prove that the marriage did *not* occur. In some states, there is still no official requirement that marriages be recorded. In addition, couples can request that these records be sealed. If you do find a marriage certificate, it will generally give you the man's name, woman's former name, residences, place and date of marriage and presiding official, religion, and the names of witnesses.

What's *Not* Public

Sometimes the personal information you might want or need most about a person is not public information. Here's a sampling of records that are generally not public. (Note that in many instances, this doesn't mean that you can't gain access to the information, simply that it's not information that anyone is legally entitled to. For more information about how to go about tracking these facts, see Chapter 6, "Other Methods of Obtaining Information.")

Personal and business income tax records: The Internal Revenue Service will generally not tell you anything more than the date that the last return was filed and the address of the business or individual. You cannot obtain copies of the actual returns.

Welfare or Social Security recipients: In certain instances, these agencies will forward a letter to someone for you, but they will not tell you who is receiving money from them or give you the address of anyone. The Social Security Administration is also not authorized to give out Social Security numbers.

Medical records: Although these records are not generally public information, the data contained within them is more accessible and gets passed around more than most of us like to admit. For example, most patients automatically fill out forms that allow their insurance company access to all medical information about them.

Going a step further, many insurance companies are hooked up to the Medical Information Bureau (MIB), a company that compiles health and medical information about individuals and then compiles a report similar to a credit report. It's estimated that one of every seven Americans is on file with this bureau.

Credit Reports: This information is not public to everyone, but there are many instances when it is legal to obtain credit information. For example, provisions of the Fair Credit Reporting Act allow you to check anyone's credit history when you have the person's permission and in certain other instances, such as when someone is applying for a credit card, loan, or credit for a business transaction. There are other ways to obtain this information, but be aware that violation of this law is punishable by a fine and possible jail time. It can also leave you open to a civil suit.

Adoption Records: These records are virtually impossible to get to without a court order. For more information about adoptions, see Chapter 8, "Adoptee/Birth Parent Searches."

3 | *Business and Property Records*

If you are doing any kind of business check or background check, the person's finances and property are often a prime consideration. The following records are what you will need to find out that information, as well as data on particular buildings, including their owners.

Property Records

These records are generally kept in a county hall of records or county courthouse, listed by a grantor/grantee index. The *grantor* is someone who sells, gives, or otherwise relinquishes something. The *grantee* is the person who receives it. You can do a search by the name of either the grantor or the grantee.

Property records are an excellent way to determine if a person is trying to minimize or exaggerate ownership. For example, someone in the midst of a divorce might be trying to hide the extent of their property holdings. On the other hand, someone trying to pass themselves off as wealthy might claim to own property that is not really theirs. Public records that can tell you about the real estate and past transactions of an individual include deeds of trust, judgments, liens, powers of attorney, and so on. Unfortunately, records such as these tend to have a long lag time; sometimes as much as eight months can pass before the information is recorded.

If you are trying to determine the amount of money paid for a piece of property, the deed will not provide that information. At least, not directly. But here's a "trick" that can help you find out: Examine the amount of money paid for tax stamps on the deed of trust, then ask the clerk how much stamps cost at the time of the deed; knowing the taxes paid on the property can help determine the price.

The same office also holds map books of every parcel of property in the city or county. You can use these books to determine who owns a particular piece of property, who the previous owner was, and who owns nearby adjacent property.

County/City Engineer

If you are looking for any kind of information about a particular building, this is the place to go. Building records here include additions, repairs, demolitions, and any other structural changes that require a permit. You can usually obtain the name(s) of the permit holder(s) and sometimes even a copy of the check used to pay the fee. (If you can obtain the check, you might also have within your possession the person's current address and phone number.)

This office also often records violations against a building (including the true owner's name, which can be helpful when ownership is in question). You might also be able to find out the officers of a corporation through this office: When a permit is granted to a corporation, the names of corporate officials are often requested.

Tax Assessor/Tax Collector

Usually part of the County Clerk's or Civil Sheriff's office, this office holds the records of anyone responsible for paying taxes on *real property*—homes, lots, business buildings, land—or *personal property*, including cars, boats, airplanes, office machinery, and mobile homes. Tax bills usually show the mailing address of the person paying the tax and the location and value of the property. As in other cases, be aware that the person who is paying the tax is not necessarily the owner of the property.

You cannot gain access to individual income tax records through this office. Another agency, called the State Tax Board, or something similar, is responsible for personal and corporate taxes. These records are generally *not* public information.

Business Records

Publicly owned corporations—those that have stock that is bought and sold in a recognized public market—are by far the easiest to get information about. By law these companies have to be listed with the federal agency called the Securities and Exchange Commission (SEC); they also have to publish an annual report for the SEC that contains details of the company's financial activities for the year. These records will also show the names of the officers and substantial stockholders.

Division of Corporations

Sometimes a separate office, sometimes part of the Secretary of State's office, this department maintains an alphabetical listing of all corporations in the state. All corporations must be registered in one of the fifty states, including all foreign companies doing any kind of business in the U.S.

For each corporation listed, you will also find information about the company's officers and directors, headquarters, and the type of business. This office also lists information about limited partnerships and lists general and limited partners by name (the county clerk's office for the place of the business usually has similar information).

State Sales Tax Board

In states where there's a sales tax on retail merchandise, the State Sales Tax Board or a similar agency handles the returns filed by businesses. These records, generally public, contain financial information about the business, such as anticipated sales and bank account numbers.

Fictitious Business Names

Records concerning fictitious business names are generally held in the county courthouse or county clerk's office. Anytime a business is using a name other than the real name of the owner, a statement must be filed. Note that banks are not permitted to open an account for someone in any name other than a legal name or an officially recorded business name. The records will tell you the fictitious business name, the owner's real name and home address, the names and addresses of any associates, ownership arrangements, and if the business is incorporated and in what state.

Internal Revenue Service

Most of their records are not public information. However, if you have the business or person's full name and a federal tax number or Social Security number, you can find out the date that the last return was filed and the address of the business or individual.

Workmen's Compensation Board

These records are kept by the state, although they are often duplicated at the county level. If you believe someone is receiving workmen's compensation, the records are worth looking at because they contain medical information and background data that is normally confidential.

Permits and Licenses

Many professionals and tradespeople are required to have a license or some sort of permit in order to practice. In many cases, the application for such a license or permit requires a lot of information about the person as well as professional and business interests; most of this information is public record. Note that licensing isn't limited to such professions as doctors and lawyers; did you know most roofers, plumbers, hairdressers, and workers in a host of other trades also require licensing?

For information about possible suits against professionals, including doctors, lawyers, and other licensed professionals, you will still need to check the appropriate court records. Generally, the associations or boards that license these individuals will not give out any information other than whether or not the person in question is actually licensed. (See Chapter 4 for information about criminal and court records.)

If, for example, you are considering suing your physician, first you would check with the medical licensing agency in your area to make sure the doctor is actually licensed. This agency will tell you whether or not the doctor is licensed, but will not inform you of any old or current malpractice suits. For this, you'll need to check the court records. If the doctor lives and works in two different counties, be sure to check both; he or she could have been served at a work address or at home. There will be a record of all cases and how they are found, including the name of the plaintiff, the docket number, and the names of the attorneys and judge. From that, you should be able to get the full records from the court's clerk, provided that there hasn't been any agreement that the records be sealed.

Following are some of the most commonly used sources of licensing and permit information.

City and County Clerk's Office, County Courthouse

This should be your first step for information about any local business. One of these offices will usually hold the permit and licensing information for businesses, including the name and address of business, owner or agent, phone numbers, type of business, number of employees, date filed, and expiration date.

Professional Licensing Bureau, State Board of Licensing

Usually in the state's capital, this office lists anyone licensed to practice any kind of profession in the state. It generally includes such occupations as physicians, chiropractors, osteopathic physicians, midwives, nurses and other medical professionals, cosmetologists, hairdressers, real estate brokers, private investigators, certified board accountants, and more.

Unfortunately, these people won't give you a lot of information: They'll merely confirm if a person has a license in good standing and an address where that license is located. It's possible you might also be able to get some other information, such as correct spelling of name, middle name, address, phone number, and perhaps other personal data. The office will not tell you about any complaints as long as the license is in good standing.

Medical Associations

Again, not a minefield of information, this office will not generally confirm anything more than whether or not someone has a license to practice and any specialties in which he or she is "board certified." Note that an M.D. does not have to be board certified to, for example, perform surgery. Also be aware that an M.D. who is certified to perform surgery might not be certified to, say, perform cosmetic surgery.

Bar Association

Don't bother looking for anything more here than if the person is a member of the state's bar and possibly an address. Complaints are generally not a matter of public record (although a lawyer convicted of a felony is automatically disbarred, which does become public information). For background information on a particular lawyer, consider checking the law journals in the county of practice to see if they have published anything or been written about for any reason.

For the Social Security number of an attorney, which can lead to access to other public records, try the Federal Courthouse. In New York City, for example, the Federal Courthouse maintains files on any attorney permitted to practice in federal court, with address, Social Security number, and sometimes a home phone number.

Federal Aviation Authority

This agency can confirm the licensing of aircraft (from its wing number) and pilots (from the name), including when the license expires. Sometimes you can also find out if a particular person owns aircraft. The aircraft itself—like a car—is considered unsecured property and therefore subject to state legislation dealing with division of property, inheritance, and legal seizure. If you know where the person resides or where the aircraft is kept, you can get more information from the local tax assessor.

Boat and Fishing Licenses

Fishers are generally licensed by a state agency called the Fish and Game Commission, or something similar, located in the state's capital. In some states, this same agency also licenses boats. In other states, the Motor Vehicle Department licenses commercial and pleasure boats and commercial and recreational fishing vessels.

Unions and Associations

In certain professions, unions and associations are the norm. While their information is not necessarily public record, you can sometimes find out more about a person through these sources. These are also a good source if you are trying to locate someone: While it probably will not give out the address of the person you are seeking, the union or association will sometimes forward a piece of mail. Many times, these organizations also have newsletters, in which you can run a classified ad requesting that a person (or anyone who knows this person) get in touch with you. Check in your local library for books listing associations, unions, and other organizations.

4 | *Criminal and Court Records*

If you are trying to find someone or obtain background information, the American court and criminal justice system just might hold the key. Cutting through the different layers of bureaucracy can be confusing for the novice, but there is a logic to the system if you persevere.

Where to Find the Records

Local and *state* court records are usually only maintained at the courthouse in which the case was tried. There is usually no central index, so it might become necessary to search all the courthouses in a particular city for the records you're seeking. In larger cities, like New York and Los Angeles, copies are also kept in one or more central storage locations. *Federal* court records are held in federal courthouses, usually in or near the county seat or state capital.

Law Enforcement Officials

These agencies, including local police departments, sheriffs' offices, and U.S. Marshall offices, are generally not your best bet for getting information. Besides the fact that their records are not public, the people who man them are generally so overworked that they don't have the time, even if they had the inclination, to help you out. If you have a real need for their records, a subpoena is the best route.

One exception to this rule is the state police and highway patrol, whose records generally *are* public information, although sometimes limited. For example, access to car accident reports might be limited to the people involved and their insurance companies. If you can get to those reports, they generally contain the names and addresses of the people involved and witnesses, license numbers, next of kin, and more. These records may be held in the state capitol, the local state office building, or the county courthouse.

Court Records

Most court records are filed by a plaintiff/defendant index. The *plaintiff* is the person who brings the suit; the *defendant* is, as the name implies, the person responsible for defending himself against the charges made.

Different courts are responsible for different kinds of matters, broadly divided into criminal and civil courts.

Criminal Courts

These courts try felony, misdemeanor, and summary cases. A *felony* is any crime from robbery to murder for which the defendant is tried by a prosecutor (a lawyer employed by the District Attorney) representing the People of the community and that is subject to punishment ranging from imprisonment of more than one year up to the death penalty. A *criminal misdemeanor*—usually such things as minor theft, simple assault, drunk driving, carrying a firearm without a license, etc.—also involves the People vs. a defendant. A *summary* case includes such offenses as disorderly conduct, public drunkenness, and retail theft (stealing from a store) under a certain amount of money.

After a case has been completed—after conviction, sentencing, and all appeals—records of convictions are open to the public. The files should include transcripts of criminal trials, which are prepared by court reporters, as well as names of witnesses, evidence, formal pleadings by prosecutors and defense counsel, judge's rulings on these pleadings, the name of the penal or mental institution to which the person is sentenced, the name of the probation officer, if probation was ordered, and more.

Civil Courts

These courts deal with disputes between individuals, and are generally citizen against citizen. Cases can involve money owed, property, child custody, and so on. Damages are usually a sum of money paid or some other reward or loss as determined by the judge or jury, as opposed to imprisonment.

The plaintiff/defendant index will only have a record of whether or not a case was filed. In order to find out the details and resolution of the suit, you will need to see the actual file, which is public information. Files are not allowed to leave the premises where they are housed, but you are permitted to make copies, either by taking notes or using a copy machine.

Nonpublic Court Records

While most court records are public information, the following are not:

- Adoption courts
- Child protection courts
- Juvenile courts

Other cases that are not public include criminal cases involving people protected by the government and cases that include what the judge deems confidential information. In certain instances, other confidential information in a case, such as bank records, credit information, and other financial background, is generally not available to the public. If necessary for legal reasons, you might be able to get access to any of the above through a court order.

Types of Courts

The following are the names of courts that are typically found across the country. All states have courts for misdemeanors, trials, felony trials, and appeals (some states also have intermediate courts of appeal). The names—and in certain instances even their corresponding functions—may vary from state to state, as will the way the county court system is set up. Here are some general guidelines for what each court handles.

Domestic Relations or Divorce Court: These courts handle divorce actions (the State Supreme Court might also handle divorces; see below). Divorce and annulment records generally include the date and place of marriage, names of children, most recent address, earlier divorces, and a description of estimation of value of jointly held property. The records are held at the courthouse where the decree was handed down, and copies are generally also sent to the state's Vital Statistics Office.

Traffic Court: This court, obviously, handles traffic violations. Their records are forwarded to the state by city, county, and state officials, where they are then filed at the Driver's License Bureau.

Small Claims Court: This court involves cases that are citizen against citizen, with no actual "crime" committed. There is usually an award limit, somewhere in the range of up to $1,500.

Municipal Court: This court generally handles criminal misdemeanors, infractions such as minor theft, battery, drunk driving, and trespassing. The damage award limits are higher than in small claims courts, but lower than in superior courts. Cases involve the People—represented by the District Attorney's office—against the defendant.

Probate Court: These courts, at the county level, handle estate matters and name changes. Estate matters include the details of the person's estate, names and addresses of those in the will, names of the executor, administrator, lawyers, children surviving and deceased, the deceased's parents, final disposition of will, and presiding court officer.

To find out if someone has legally changed their name, you can look up whichever name you have—either the old one or the new one. Cases are listed under both names, as well as by the year of the change; the reasons for the name change are usually not given.

State Superior Court: Both felony and civil cases are tried in this court, usually involving sums of more than $10,000 with no upper limits on damage awards.

State Supreme Court: This court generally handles appeals from the State Superior Court and usually has the records of divorces, although sometimes the domestic relations court also handles this matter. The information about divorces that you can obtain varies from state to state: In some states, you might be entitled to the entire file; in others, you might only have access to an index number, judge of record, attorneys of record, and the date the divorce decree was final.

Federal Bankruptcy Court: Any kind of bankruptcy must be filed with this court, although there are several different kinds of bankruptcies, including:

- *Chapter 7*: bankruptcies for individuals, partnerships, and corporations
- *Chapter 11*: reorganization for partnerships and corporations
- *Chapter 13*: temporary relief from creditors, for individuals only

Available information might include the full name, address, net worth when filing, business name and kind, spouse name, age, and occupation.

Federal Civil Court: These courts handle all federal civil matters and those related to lawsuits involving federal regulatory agencies such as the ICC, FCC, etc., including copyrights.

Federal Criminal Court: Although most criminal charges are handled in state courts—because most felonies (murder, rape, assault, etc.) are state matters—there are certain instances when these matters are handled in the federal court system. They include those crimes committed on federal land—such as military land, a reservation, or VA hospital. Other federal crimes tried in this court include kidnapping across state lines, racketeering, mail, wire, and securities fraud, drug smuggling, and most crimes involving interstate commerce.

5 | *Other Methods of Obtaining Information*

As discussed, public records are a prime way of getting almost any kind of information about somebody. But these records won't tell you *everything* about a person. What do you do if you need or want more information than is available in the public records? Here are some of the methods the professionals employ. Some of these you can use yourself; for others, it's best to employ the services of a private investigator.

Remember that under *no* circumstances is an individual allowed to portray him- or herself as a private investigator if that's not really the case—*it's against the law and you will get caught.* Enough said. Also remember that you cannot—ever—represent yourself as any kind of government agent, law enforcement official, or member of the clergy. As for other kinds of misrepresentation, such as "stretching" the truth—you know yourself how much you feel comfortable with.

If you're not comfortable not telling the truth, try this: Simply don't say who you are and let people make their own assumptions. Here's how it works: Say you want to find out if someone is an illegal alien. You could go to the person's employer and start asking authoritative questions about that person's immigration status. If you do it with enough confidence, most people will not question your right to be asking questions.

Not sure it's that easy? Well, it is; I've done it. In fact, in one case, I was later accused of misrepresenting myself to the person I had questioned. However, I was able to explain that not only had I *not* misrepresented myself, I had never even identified myself with anything more than a first name! I asked questions and he answered. There were no further problems.

The Trash Pickers

Never had the desire to be a trash collector? Maybe it's time to think again. What can you get digging through someone's trash? Just about everything!

The Phone Bill

Need a person's phone number to get to their public records? Many people just throw out their phone bill after it's paid. There, right at the top of each page, will be the phone number.

And neatly lined up along the pages will be a record of every long-distance phone call made that month. Suspect your boyfriend still speaks to his ex-girlfriend in another city? Check that bill—the phone number will be there in black and white if he does. As will the phone number of the competing company that you think your business partner is considering merging with behind your back, the phone number of your missing ex-spouse who isn't paying child support even though your ex-mother-in-law claims not to know where he's moved, the phone number of...whoever the person is talking to long distance.

What do you do once you have the long distance phone numbers? Two options: One is a *reverse phone book*. Look in your local library for the *Cole's Directory*, which lists phone numbers and gives you the person's name from the phone number. As long as the phone number is listed, you can look it up in one of these books and find out the address and name of the person living there. If you want, you can then double-check that information by using the *Haines Criss-Cross Directory*, which lists street addresses and their occupants.

Option number two is to pick up your own telephone and start talking. If you suspect you know whose phone number it is that you're calling, your job is easy: Simply ask to speak with that person. If not, here's your chance to be "creative." Think about the times you might have given out your name over the phone. What induced *you* to give out that information? Chances are the same thing will persuade others to give their names, such as a phone survey, confirmation of records, a call to make sure some service is being performed correctly, etc. Use your imagination!

What you usually can't find out from a phone bill is the local numbers that have been called, because they are not broken down on the average phone bill. The phone company does have a record of those calls, however, and they are available to any customer for the customer's own telephone number (although the phone company doesn't particularly like to give out that information). The easiest way to find out who's being called locally is to make friends with someone at the telephone company or to tap the telephone (see "Electronic Surveillance" below).

Credit Card Bills and Receipts

In the past, credit cards were used mostly to pay for the big-ticket items, but more and more, people use them to pay their everyday expenses as well. Receipts and bills can show anything from the purchase of a carton of cigarettes to the week's food bill, from payment of restaurant dinners to hotel rooms, from charges for a short taxi fare to international airline flights.

At worst, these records will show you which credit cards the person has and how he or she tends to use them. At best, they can hold the answer to all your questions.

Personal Letters and Notes

Unless your subject is a major pack rat, most letters, birthday cards, and the like will eventually end up in the trash can. I can't even begin to predict what information you might find in these items! Likewise, notes and to-do lists can give you the key to what the person has been doing on a daily basis and possibly even what is planned for the future.

Bank Statements and Other Financial Information

Not only will these tell you how much money the person has, and where it is, but it will also give you account numbers in case you need to do further checking. Other similar items include statements of interest, loan statements, stock or bond statements, tax assessments for property, etc.

Miscellaneous Trash

Who knows what else you can learn from a person's garbage that can be worthwhile. Finding low-calorie frozen food boxes might lead you to check local exercise clubs for a membership. A school catalog might indicate a person is taking classes in something. Birth control packages or other medicine can give you an idea of daily habits and health problems. Magazines and books indicate the subjects the person is interested in.

Surveillance

First things first: Unless it's raining, forget the trench coat. The number-one rule of surveillance—which is just a fancy name for watching everything someone does—is to blend in with your environment. If you're following a stockbroker, you'd better be dressed like a stockbroker, likewise if you're following a construction worker, you'd better look like one.

Why? The first reason is you don't want to look obvious—either to the person you're following or to anyone else. For example, when your stockbroker walks into his office building, steps into the elevator, and gets off at a certain floor, you can be following right behind—as long as you look like you belong there. But if you're wearing jeans and a T shirt, someone will either stop you or at the very least notice you.

Blending into an environment isn't just limited to clothing. You should also make sure you have the right car, the right attitude, even the right physical characteristics. (A white person hanging around in a Hispanic neighborhood is going to get noticed, as will a male on an all-female college campus, and so on.) If you don't have the right look yourself, find someone who does.

Surveillance can be very time-consuming and—honestly—not all that exciting. You'll probably spend most of your time waiting for the person to actually *do* something. Before you start any kind of surveillance, try to get an idea of the neighborhood you'll be in and what might come up during the hours you'll be there. Does a local school let out in the mid-afternoon, either creating confusion or reducing the speed limit on that road? Is there a massive influx of people into the area at 5:30 P.M. as residents return home from work? Or maybe the streets are packed with joggers at 6:30 A.M. Having an idea of what normally goes on in the neighborhood can help prevent surprises that could lead to your losing the person you're trying to watch. Along the same lines, try to get a clear idea of what the person's schedule normally entails to eliminate as many surprises as possible.

It's not against the law to simply follow a person as long as you keep a "reasonable" distance between yourself and the person you're following. Any individual has what's generally considered a reasonable right to privacy, but when a person is in a public place, anyone else has the same right to be there. If, however, a person knows that they're being followed, they could consider it "harassment" or even "stalking" and make a complaint to the police.

For example, once my company was following a man for sixty-two days. Even though we changed the teams of people watching him, it eventually became clear to him that he was being followed. (He was being prosecuted by the Singapore government for crimes committed there, so he had an idea he was going to be followed anyway.) At first, it didn't seem to bother him, but eventually he did bring the FBI in on it. We were told that keeping a "loose" tail would be OK, but if we got too close to the subject, they might have to entertain his complaint and consider what we were doing harassment.

Automobile surveillance is by far the most difficult kind since most drivers make a habit of constantly checking their rearview and side mirrors. Make sure the car you're driving is unobtrusive, which in most cases means leaving the shiny red Porsche and the beaten up 1967 Chevy at home. The rule in my company is to keep to the right and rear of the vehicle you're following—basically the blind side. Alternate, though, so it doesn't become too obvious that you're following. Consider, for example, getting ahead of the car you're following for short periods of time when you're fairly sure it won't be making any sudden turnoffs.

Of course, if you're not sure where the person is going, the chances of them making some unanticipated move are that much greater, so you'll have to really pay attention. Some other tips: Make sure you have plenty of change for tolls and invest in a car phone in case you get into any kind of trouble.

Surveillance in a residential area can also get pretty tricky. If you think you can just park your car in front of the person's house and wait there all day without anyone noticing, think again. Even if the person you're watching doesn't notice, someone else will—this is even truer in upscale neighborhoods—and you'll soon find the police knocking at your car window. If you have a "legitimate" reason for watching the person, consider informing the police ahead of time that you are going to be in the area. A licensed investigator will usually inform the police when doing this kind of surveillance so as not to get hassled by patrol cars.

Licensed investigators can also use less obtrusive methods for this kind of surveillance. For example, we often rent a used van with markings on it of some sort of utility company, appliance company, or plumbing company. The person in the truck dresses accordingly, and no one is ever the wiser.

One last tip: Try to pair up with another person when doing surveillance, especially if you are trying to follow a couple. In such a case, a male and female is best so that if the man and woman you're following split up, say to go to the restrooms, you can each follow one of them.

If you think you might need to do surveillance in the future, there's an easy way to practice. Go to any busy place and randomly pick a person to follow. See how long you can follow before you are noticed. Also see how far away you can stay without losing the person and how close you can get without calling attention to yourself. This will give you the opportunity to experience firsthand what kinds of obstacles you might run into before it really counts.

Electronic Surveillance

Room bugs and video cameras are no longer the stuff of futuristic, Orwellian versions of the world—they are here now. While following a subject personally is still the preferred method on television—and the only accessible way for most individuals—there are many times when private investigators prefer to enter the high-tech arena.

The technology changes so quickly it's almost impossible to be completely up-to-date, but here are the basics. Telephone bugs and room bugs are alive and well, and not all that expensive or even that difficult to install, if you know what you're doing. In fact, there are certain kinds of telephone taps where no access to the actual telephone is even required (just access to the telephone lines).

If you think there's a chance that someone's tapping your phone, there are devices you can buy to prevent the transmission. Usually as soon as a product comes out, though, it's not long before another one capable of stopping it is also brought onto the market. It can quickly turn into a game of who has the most high-tech equipment. For example, one sophisticated form of bugging involves a laser-beam gun that can be pointed at a window up to 1,500 feet away and pick up conversations from the room inside from the vibrations of the glass. The method to prevent this? Silver foil over the windows!

Be aware, too, that information gained through a telephone tap or the recording of a conversation is often not admissible in court; in fact, in many states, it's illegal altogether. The laws vary by state, but for the most part, it's illegal to record conversations unless you have a court order or are a party to the conversation. If you're considering some form of recording, be sure to check the laws in your state. You might still decide to go ahead and record, knowing that you'll have to confirm any information you gain by other methods.

As for video cameras, they range from full-fledged systems that can look into any apartment in a building to hand-held mini-cameras that can be carried on your body and even cameras in small items, like the kind Maxwell Smart used to carry. In other words, there's a camera for any need—as long as you can get in to set it up or close enough to use it.

If you can't get that close, there are remote video cameras that can be used. For example, you can set up a video camera with a telescopic zoom lens in the taillight of a nearby car, with the heavy equipment in the car's trunk. Then the camera gets hooked up to a remote video cassette recorder and microwave relay station that investigators can monitor from a distant point.

Any recorder used should have a time and date generator, which records and allows the viewer to see the date and time on the screen—and also allows the tape to be used as evidence if necessary.

Going Undercover

This isn't something you're really going to be able to do yourself; for the most part, if undercover work is needed, it's best to hire a professional. Here's what's involved: A person (again, usually a licensed investigator) enters a situation where they pretend to be someone they're not. It's easiest to understand with an example. My company was hired once by a company that believed one of its employees was selling drugs. The person they suspected was a stockbroker. We put in an investigator who had some experience in stocks. He worked as a stockbroker, all the while keeping an eye on, and becoming friendly with, the suspected person. It wasn't long before we had the evidence we needed that this person was indeed selling drugs. (As often happens, he was fired rather than prosecuted because of the time, money, and possible bad publicity involved in pressing charges.)

As you can see, the qualifications of the person going undercover are critical. The person must appear to fit in with the rest of the environment. Ideally, they should have a real knowledge of whatever it is they're going to be called upon to do. In addition, they should do an extensive background check on the company and other people they're going to be with (as long as they remember that they're not supposed to know anything about these other people when they meet!).

If you're interested in getting into undercover work yourself, you should know that while undercover investigations can be a lot of fun and exciting, the people who do them are typically paid less for it than for other investigative work. Most often, their jobs involve working in a department store or a supermarket, watching other employees.

Inside Contacts

Wouldn't it be nice to just pick up the phone and say "OK, Mack, whadda ya got on this guy?" Well, to some extent you can—if you know the right people. Who are the "right people"? That depends on what it is you need to know.

The obvious answer starts with a friend on the police force, but you might not be able to get as much information from the police as you think. Yes, police do have access to all sorts of wonderful computer records. No, they're not allowed to just access it for any reason. In most cases, if they're doing, say, a criminal record search, they need to enter their own badge number or some other form of identification. Use can be subject to fairly intense scrutiny; if it turns out records are being searched for any kind of business other than official, the person doing you a favor could end up in a lot of trouble.

So who else is worth knowing? Generally people who work in banks or other financial institutions can provide a lot of information about the financial status of people you're interested in. Better yet, they also have access to credit ratings, which contain a wealth of information, including address, phone number, Social Security number, and so on. Contacts at credit card companies and local utility companies can also pull records that reveal a lot about the lifestyle of the person you need to know about.

Besides that, you'll need to do some digging to come up with your own list of who might be able to help in certain situations: maybe an editor who has access to computer databases, a real estate agent who has the key to the building a subject lives in, a waitress who can casually listen to some conversations, someone from the phone company who could check out the local calls a subject makes, a cable customer service person who can look up the records and give you someone's address. The list is endless.

Often, these contacts don't have to be friends—just people who you meet along the way. Recently a casual conversation with a cab driver led to my hiring him for the day to do some work for my company. I keep a constantly updated phone book with the names of everyone I meet and their occupation for just such cases. You never know whose knowledge will come in handy.

6 | *Using Information Brokers and Hiring Private Investigators*

All the public records listed so far are records you can obtain on your own. Some are accessible through the mail; for others, you actually have to go to the proper office in person. But what if you don't have the time to check every courthouse in your area? Or the money to fly to and stay in another state while you do your search? Or the connections to obtain information you need that isn't part of the public records?

If you own or have access to a computer, one alternative is to use an *information broker*, sometimes called an *information supplier*. Basically, these companies are wholesalers of information: They obtain the information from databases and then pass it on to you, the customer, at a profit.

These companies can work in a couple of different ways. With some, you need an account to begin with and then pay a fee each time you access information. Others will ask you to pay only when you access the information, without an initial setup fee.

Using Information Brokers

Following is a brief description of some of the better-known companies. With computers and computer services becoming ever more popular, new companies are springing up all the time. Note, too, that some of these companies will only work with licensed private investigators. Before agreeing to work with any particular company, ask it to send you any literature that they have available and be sure to ask questions before you sign on.

Be aware that dealing with any one of these companies will probably not be cheap. They can, however, be incredible time-savers, and in certain cases, it will be cheaper than doing the research yourself. Your best bet for keeping costs down is to know exactly what you're looking for and to do as much as possible of the initial search yourself.

AT&T Easy Link
1 Lake Street
Upper Saddle River, New Jersey 07458
(800) 435-7375

This is a worldwide electronic communication service that gives your computer access to databases in such categories as accounting, agriculture, annual reports, banking and finance, articles from magazines and books, and more.

CDB Infotek
P. O. Box 5466
Orange, California
92613-5466
(800) 427-3747

You will need a computer and modem to access any regional and national investigative public records information. Samples include credit bureau information, publisher's mailing lists, telephone directories, motor vehicle ownership searches, bankruptcy filings, Social Security number tracks, and driving histories.

Information Resource Services Company (IRSC)
3777 N. Harbor Boulevard
Fullerton, California 92635
(800) 640-4772

This company is connected to 700 national and international databases. It supplies public records. You must have an account with them, and a computer modem. They can supply information about identifying, locating, and background. Possibilities include information from records, including driver's licenses, real property, assets, fictitious business names, marriage and death, voter registration, and more.

Prentice Hall

500 Central Avenue
Albany New York 12206
(800) 333-0431

This service is useful for worldwide public record information searches, including records pertaining to secured transactions, SEC and federal agencies, court records, corporate services, asset/lien search services, environmental searches, and special services such as patent and trademark searches, mortgage searches, and grantee/grantor searches.

TRW Redi Property Data

1700 Northwest 66th Avenue
Fort Lauderdale, Florida 33313
(800) 327-1072

This company can hook you up with real estate information in most parts of the United States. Note that the data is updated every six months to a year, and the information can change in that time. In other words, just because you don't find a transaction listed here doesn't mean it didn't happen. Make sure you do verify any information you obtain through other sources.

U.S. Datalink

6711 Bayway Drive
Baytown, Texas 77520
(800) 527-7930

This service is similar to the above companies, with a variety of public records searches available.

Hiring a Private Investigator

Even with the aid of information brokers, there are times when you are going to need more help in your search for information. Maybe you've gone through all the public records and still haven't found the information you're looking for. Maybe you've just gone as far as you can on your own and need some help.

While fees vary depending on the exact nature of the work, you can expect to pay anywhere from several hundred to several thousand dollars. For this reason, even if you are going to hire a private detective, doing some of the upfront work yourself can end up saving you a lot of money in the long run. The logical time to turn to the private investigator is when you have already gone as far as you can on your own.

Private investigators have networks of contacts that can supply them information that the average citizen just doesn't have access to. They are also experienced in using legal subterfuge to gain information and have the equipment and expertise for surveillance and other tactics used to find out information.

Where do you find one? As is the case when you're hiring anyone, a reference from someone who has used a particular investigator and been pleased with the result is always the best bet. But there's a good chance that you don't know anyone who has hired a private detective. (And even if you do, there's a good chance that you don't know it. It's not the kind of information people tend to offer up casually at cocktail parties!)

Start with the Yellow Pages to find listings of private investigators. As in any profession, private investigators come in a mix of the good, the bad, and the ugly. How can you make sure you're getting one of the good ones?

Rule number one is don't be intimidated by private investigators. Remember, you're the one doing the hiring and you have the right to know what you're getting into ahead of time. If you are unsure or nervous about working with a particular person or company, move onto the next one on your list. Here are some questions to ask:

1. Are you licensed? In what state(s)?
2. How many years have you been a licensed investigator?
3. Do you specialize in any particular kinds of cases?
4. Can you handle this assignment?
5. What kind of similar experience do you have?
6. When can you begin work?
7. How often will you make reports? What kind of reports (oral, written) and what will they include?
8. What is your fee structure?
9. Are there ever any extra charges? For what?
10. Do you require a deposit and/or a retainer?

As a client, you too have certain responsibilities. Before you contact anyone, give some thought to the following:

1. Make sure your objective is clear in your own mind.
2. Know how much you are willing and able to pay for the investigator's services.
3. Be prepared to tell the investigator *all* relevant information.
4. Respond promptly to any calls or correspondence from the investigator and make payment(s) promptly.

Part II
Kinds of Searches

7 | *How to Find Anyone*

Regardless of the reason why, when someone asks me to find a person for them, I always ask them some basic questions. See how many of these questions you can answer now about the person you are looking for:

1. Do you have the full name?
2. Do you have the last known address?
3. Do you know the date of birth?
4. Do you know the Social Security number?
5. Does he or she drive?
6. Do you know where the person works(ed)?
7. Do you know what kind of business the person is in?
8. Do you have an old or current phone number?
9. Do you know if the person has any family?
10. Do you have any telephone numbers of friends or relatives in another state or area code?
11. Can you give me a complete description of the individual?

If you can't answer these questions now, start searching your memory and your records. The answers to most of the above questions can be found through public records, but why waste your time if you already have them? Once you've gathered all the information you do have, it's time to map out your game plan.

What Kind of Search Is It?

Who you are looking for and why can determine to some extent how you will conduct your search. There are basically two kinds of searches: "friendly" and "not friendly."

Chances are your search falls into the "friendly" category: an old lover, a high school friend for a reunion, a relative who has inherited money, the person who owns a business or piece of property that you are interested in purchasing, and so on. These searches are generally the easiest to conduct because the person you are looking for probably will want to be found once they realize you're searching. And people you encounter along the way will probably be more than happy to help you in your quest.

An "unfriendly" search can be more difficult because it generally involves a person who doesn't want to be found. A father who is delinquent in child support, an ex-lover who took off with all your possessions, or the person who bilked you out of your life savings is certainly going to avoid you at all costs.

Other searches can fall somewhere between those two categories, most notably searches for missing people (even when your intent is friendly, it can be difficult to track people who have "run away" or involuntarily been "taken away") and searches involving adoption. Whether your search is for a child given up for adoption or for a birth parent, current laws are set up to discourage you as much as possible. Even if the child and parent are looking for each other, it takes a lot of time, perseverance, and sometimes just plain luck.

Before I go into these special situations, here are some of the general steps to take when looking for anyone. In most instances, you will use a combination of public records and other techniques to find the person in question. The following steps are only a guideline—every search will go off in its own direction and you have to be prepared to run with whatever information you come up with. Special situations and examples are covered at the end of this chapter and in the following chapters.

General Search Guidelines

If you're looking for someone whose name and general whereabouts you already know, start at the very beginning—with the phone book. Granted, most cases take more work than simply opening the White Pages, but wouldn't it be frustrating to search all sorts of public records only to find out the answer was already in your living room?

Even if you haven't seen someone in twenty years and have no idea where he or she might be living now, start with the phone book for the area of their last known address. Although people move around more than ever these days, many people never leave their hometown or the first place they settle as adults.

To obtain a phone number outside of your area, simply check the White Pages for the area you are interested in—local libraries generally have a selection of phone books available for public use. Or, if you're willing to spend a couple cents more for the ease of not leaving your home, call Information for that area (the area code and 555-1212). If you don't know the area code, you can obtain it from your local Information operator. From Information or the telephone book, you can also obtain the person's address if it is listed. Call your local post office for the area's zip code.

Assuming that the phone book doesn't yield any information that you can use, the next step I normally take is to check with the Board of Elections to see if the person is a registered voter. Note that any one of the following steps might provide a current address. If it does, congratulations, you're done! If not, it might at least provide a previous address, from which you can obtain a present address. Or you might have to move on to the next step.

Board of Elections information is a natural starting place because the information is readily accessible and easy to obtain—and it provides a lot of information, including date of birth, address, telephone number, employment, and so on. (For a full listing of what kind of information contained in this and other public records and methods discussed in this chapter, go back to Chapters 2 through 6.)

From here, you can try a motor vehicle search, which generally provides an address. Once you have that address, you can search the property records in the given county to determine if the person rents (or rented) or owns (or owned) the property. If it is rented, you might be able to get some information from the landlord, including a forwarding address or place of employment if the person has left that address. You can also fill out a Freedom of Information request at the Post Office for a forwarding address if the person has moved within the past year.

Another vital piece of information a landlord might have is the Social Security number of the person you are looking for. (It might be on the lease or obtainable because of a legal requirement that the landlord have the tenant's Social Security number for income tax purposes if there is a security deposit). You might also be able to obtain the Social Security number through the top portion of a credit report. While credit reports as a whole are not public information, the top portion is, and contains the person's name, address, Social Security number, employer, and date of birth (just the month and year, not the exact date). The first three digits of a person's Social Security number tell you in which state the number was issued, a logical starting point for a search for other public records. (See Appendix A for a breakdown by state of Social Security numbers.)

If you have been able to find out the person's business or occupation, you can check with the various licensing departments to see if they are still licensed in that particular area. If you have discovered the individual's previous employer, the previous employer might be able to tell you the current employer.

As you can see from the above, you'll have to be flexible when you are doing any kind of search. Seemingly unimportant information can sometimes lead you directly to the person you're searching for, while sometimes the most promising of leads only results in a dead end.

The Armed Forces

If the person you are looking for is, or was, in any branch of the armed forces, you have a good chance of success because all branches now have computerized locator services. Contact the appropriate office below.

U.S. Army
Worldwide Locator
U.S. Army Enlisted Records and Evaluation Center
Fort Benjamin Harrison, Indiana 46249-5301
(317) 542-4211

U.S. Air Force
Air Force Military Personnel Center
Worldwide Locator
Randolph AFB, Texas 78150
(210) 652-5775

U.S. Navy
Navy Locator Service
Navy Annex Building
Washington, D.C. 20370
(703) 614-3155

U.S. Marine Corps
USMC CMC
HQMC MMSB-10
2008 Elliot Road, Suite 201
Quantico, Virginia 22134-5030
(703) 640-3942

U.S. Coast Guard
Commander MPC-s
Military Personnel Command
2100 2nd Street, S.W.
Washington, D.C. 20593-0001
(202) 267-1340

Retired Military and Civil Service Personnel
The Office of Personnel Management
1900 E. Street, S.W.
Washington, D.C. 20415

Friendly Searches

There are a variety of methods you can use for a "friendly" search that don't involve public records *if* you can convince other people that you have a legitimate "good" reason for wanting to get in touch with someone. Note that these techniques can also be used to find people who might not want you to find them—if you are willing to stretch the truth somewhat when talking to other people.

Almost all adult Americans have a Social Security number. The *U.S. Social Security Administration* has the home address of anyone receiving compensation from them (such as Social Security Insurance) and the business address of all people who are legally employed. No, they won't give you another person's Social Security number or address, but they will generally forward mail to an individual if you can provide the person's name, date of birth, and a satisfactory reason why you want to get in touch. For more information, write to: U.S. Social Security Administration, OCRO, Division of Certification and Coverage, 300 North Greene Street, Baltimore, Maryland 21201.

If for some reason, the Social Security Administration cannot forward a letter, consider other agencies that might have the person's address, such as the Veteran's Administration, a particular state's vital statistics office, or even the person's insurance company (even people who move all over the country tend to stay with the same insurance company). Again, none of these agencies or companies will actually give you an address for the person you are seeking, but they should be willing to forward mail to that person if they can. For your own piece of mind, consider including a self-addressed, stamped postcard that can be sent back to you indicating whether or not they were able to fulfill your request.

If you know of any friends, relatives, former neighbors, or former coworkers of the person you are seeking, get in touch with them. Unless the person has some reason for intentionally disappearing, someone should know where they are. Of course, convincing a stranger to tell you is another matter. Unless they know or remember you themselves, it's not likely anyone is going to give out a phone number or address to a complete stranger, no matter how convincing your story. If you suspect someone does know the whereabouts of the person you are looking for (or if a person actually comes out and says so, but refuses to tell you), ask the intermediary to have the person get in touch with you. Leave your name and address and/or phone number; also consider asking them to tell the person you are seeking that it's OK to call you collect.

Even if you don't know anyone who might know the location of the person you're looking for, you might be able to track your subject down fairly easily. Say you are looking for someone with the name "Ken Bolton" whom you know last lived in Philadelphia. You check the phone book and there's no one by that name listed. But there is a Carol Bolton listed. Try giving her a call; first ask for Ken Bolton. Chances are there won't be a Ken Bolton there. But she might volunteer the information that he is her son or nephew or whatever. Even if she doesn't, feel free to come right out and ask her if she knows him. Of course, this approach is a lot easier with the last name Bolton than with the last name Smith, but it's generally worthwhile if you have good reason to believe that other family members live in a certain area.

Here are some other resources you can tap into for a friendly search:

• **Schools and Universities:** Most colleges and universities have alumni associations through which you might be able to get a current or at least the last known address. High schools also sometimes have an up-to-date record of students; if the school itself doesn't, it might be able to put you in touch with the person responsible for the last reunion.

• **Reverse Directories:** Look in your local library for these reverse phone books. The *Haines Criss-Cross Directory* lists street addresses with corresponding tenants (if you have an old address, the current resident might be able to tell you where the person you are seeking has moved to). The *Cole's Directory* lists phone numbers and gives you the person's name from the phone number.

• **Newspaper and Magazine Personals:** If you have some idea what part of the country the person might be in or know what the person is likely to read in the way of magazines or newspapers, a classified ad might be worth a chance. If you go this route, consider getting a P. O. Box for return mail—even if you do get a response from the person you are looking for, you might also get a healthy number of responses from other people who have nothing better to do with their time—and these are not the kind of people you want to know your home address! Check the *Ayer Directory of Publications* (in your local library) for nationwide listings.

• **Unions and Professional Associations:** In certain professions, unions and associations are the norm. Chances are good that if the person you are looking for was a doctor or teacher twenty years ago, they still are and might belong to a national union or association. Again, you can try asking for a letter to be forwarded to the individual, or the union or association might have its own newsletter with a classified section.

Missing People

Every year in the United States, thousands of people—adults and children—disappear. Some people intentionally leave home without a trace, such as men who leave in the face of bankruptcy or fathers who flee in an effort to avoid paying child support. While traditionally the fleeing adult has been a man, more and more women are "running away from home." Women, for the most part, are fleeing an undesirable or dangerous domestic situation rather than the financial obligations that tend to set men going. Teenagers leave voluntarily for a variety of reasons, ranging from an unhealthy or dangerous family life to a drug or alcohol problem to a need to test their wings.

The second category includes people who are taken or held against their will. Reports abound of children who are "snatched," sometimes by strangers, sometimes by a parent. Teenagers and adults, too, can be taken—kidnapped—and, worst case scenario, murdered.

While no one really wants to consider the possibility that the person they're looking for is dead, it must be considered. Deaths of identified bodies are recorded (see Chapter 2, "Basic Public Records," for more information about death records), but a surprising number of deaths are never recorded because the bodies are never found or identified.

Police departments and other law enforcement officials are notoriously unhelpful when it comes to tracking down—or even acknowledging—missing adults. When a mentally stable adult is reported missing, it is most often assumed that person left voluntarily—even when family members and friends are certain that is not the case. Even in suspicious cases, time is a factor—often the police just don't have enough time to do all the work involved in a full scale search unless they have a real and compelling reason to believe some sort of foul play has occurred. In many instances, it is up to concerned friends and family to conduct the search.

To find adults who are voluntarily missing, much the same steps are taken as in the search for anyone else. By necessity, subterfuge tends to play more of a role in these searches. For example, friends of your ex-husband who isn't paying his child support would be much more likely to tell you where he is if they thought he had inherited some money than if they thought you were going after the back payments. If you don't think you can, or want to, undertake such a search, consider hiring a private investigator experienced in collecting such information. Again, if you do decide to hire someone, you can still do much of the paper-trail work yourself, probably saving a substantial bit of money in the process.

In the particular case above, you should also know about the Federal Office of Child Support Enforcement, a part of the U.S. Department of Health and Human Services. The purpose of this office is to help collect funds due in child support from delinquent parents. Possibilities include intercepting tax-refund checks, mandatory income withholding, and liens against property and other securities. Every state has its own version of this office. For more information, contact your local office either through the District Attorney's office or the Welfare Department.

What if the person you are looking for has changed his or her name to prevent being found? First, some facts. Changing your name is not as easy as it appears to be on television. If it's a legal name change there will be a public record of the change (check the Probate Court). All legal employers require a variety of information and verification when hiring, such as a Social Security number for tax purposes and documentation to prove citizenship. If an individual does manage to obtain false documentation (yes, for the right price, it can be done), there's still the matter of a resume and verifiable references. And always the chance that the malefactor will be found out.

All in all, name changing is a risky game that most people don't have the funds—or the stomach—to undertake. This is not to say that name changing never happens. Honestly, tracking someone who has a changed name will be difficult, if not downright impossible. Fortunately, most people don't change their names, so unless you have reason to believe otherwise, start with the assumption that the person you are seeking is still using the same name.

Your first step with involuntarily missing adults or children is your local police. They should immediately enter the person's name in the National Crime Information Center (NCIC), a computerized system of storing and retrieving crime information maintained by the Federal Bureau of Investigation (FBI) in Washington, D.C. Police departments and other law enforcement agencies are tied into this system, providing a nationwide computer database. Your local police *must* list missing children and retarded and elderly adults immediately; for other adults, there must be a reasonable suspicion of some sort of foul play before they are listed. If, for any reason, the local police can't or won't enter the name of a missing child, parents can go directly to the nearest FBI office to have it listed with the NCIC.

Another resource for parents of missing children is the National Center for Missing and Exploited Children, a nonprofit clearinghouse that collects, compiles, disseminates, and exchanges information on missing children. Contact them at 2101 Wilson Boulevard, Suite 550, Arlington, Virginia 22201-3052; (800) 843-5678 or (703) 235-3900. Many states also have their own hotlines and support groups for parents of missing children. In addition, if you suspect your child has run away, try the National Runaway Hotline at (800) 621-4000; local support groups can provide information and resources to the parents of runaways.

8 | *Adoptee/Birth Parent Searches*

The search for either a child given up for adoption or the natural birth parent(s) is among the most difficult of any, mostly because the laws in most states are set up to discourage finding out such information. Public records are of virtually no help at the beginning of a search, although they can help after you obtain the initial information you are looking for. (Two states—Alabama and Kansas—do have open adoption records.) For the most part, though, true "detective" work is called for.

If you are considering such a search, please be aware of your own motives and expectations before you start. These can include the natural desire to know what has happened to your child or the kind of family you came from, as well as compelling medical reasons for the person seeking his or her birth parents. Adopted children are most often likely to want to know about their backgrounds as they approach key life events: marriage, birth of a child, death of an adoptive parent.

Also be aware that the person you are looking for might not want to be found: An adopted child might resent the intrusion of a birth parent years later; a birth parent might have built a life that has no room for a grown child. On the other hand, the person you are seeking might just as eagerly be looking for you.

What else can you expect? How about hot leads that turn

cold, promising information that leads nowhere, dead ends, and failed and mistaken memories? Add to that the rush of exhilaration when a lead does pan out, a truer sense of your own identity and history, and the ultimate sense of recognition when you finally meet your family member. In all, a lot of highs and lows. The point is that there is just no way to know what will happen, but you must be prepared for any eventuality. Still want to look? Read on.

The Birth Certificate

Birth records—which generally contain a wealth of information about a person and their background—are public information and usually available to anyone. Except for adopted children.

In the case of adoptions, the court seals the original birth certificate on the day the adoption is final. Thereafter it can only be opened by court order—which doesn't happen all that often. In place of the original birth certificate, adoptees receive an *amended birth certificate*, which does not have any identifying information such as the names of the natural parents or place of birth. This is what you will receive if you request your birth records.

It does, however, contain one piece of information that can be helpful: Every newborn is given an official number that is filed by date of birth in the county registry. In most counties, that number is *not* changed on the amended birth certificate. If you know that number and your exact birth date, it's sometimes possible to match up birth records to identify the natural birth name and parents of the child, but don't count on it.

Gather Clues

Before you start, compile any information that you do know, no matter how apparently irrelevant. Adoptees should think especially of any "slips" their adoptive parents might have made along the way: Did they ever mention the names of your mother or father? The name of a hospital, orphanage, lawyer, or birth town? A comment about how your hair was the same color as your father's or how sad it was that your mother got pregnant before she finished high school? You never know when a seemingly innocuous comment will fill in some of the holes.

If your adoptive parents are still alive—and willing—ask them now if they know anything about your natural parents or the circumstances of your birth. If not, talk to relatives and friends of your parents who might have been around at the time. Older sisters and brothers can be an especially good source of information because parents often speak openly in front of children, not realizing that the children are indeed listening and retaining what they hear. With adoptive parents, relatives, or friends, be prepared for a certain resistance and quite possibly fear. Explaining your personal reasons for your search may help break down any initial reluctance.

Birth mothers and fathers should also record any similar information: Was there any contact with the adoptive parents? Did you meet them or hear that they were a fine family from the Midwest? Do you know they already had two older daughters or were unable to have children of their own?

Support Groups

As searches become more and more prevalent, so too have support groups and organizations designed to provide information and aid in the searches. The following are national organizations and resources that can help with your search.

Adoptees Liberty Movement Association (ALMA)
P. O. Box 727
Radio City Station

New York, New York 10101-0727
(212) 581-1568

For a tax-deductible membership fee ($64 at press time), this group provides search assistance, support groups, a handbook, and a listing in its reunion registry which features 800,000 names.

Adoption Search Institute
P. O. Box 11749
Costa Mesa, California 92627

This organization provides classes and information about how to efficiently conduct a search.

American Adoption Congress
1000 Connecticut Avenue, N.W., Suite 9
Washington, D.C. 20036

This group will supply a list of search support groups, search consultants, and psychotherapists in your state free of charge if you include a stamped self-addressed envelope.

International Soundex Reunion Registry
P.O. Box 2312
Carson City, Nevada 89702

This organization helps adoptees, birth parents, siblings, and other family members find each other. Registration is free. Send stamped self-addressed envelope for more information.

In addition to the national organizations, many states have state search groups and registries that can provide practical and emotional help to searchers. The national organizations above can point you in the right direction. So far, twenty-two states have set up their own voluntary registries to match birth parents with adoptees.

Also check your local library and bookstore for books dedicated to the birth parent/adopted child search. The Kammandale Library, in St. Paul, Minnesota, holds more

than 35,000 books on topics related to any kind of family
search, such as adoptees and birth parents, background,
genealogical information, nationality, inheritance, and
more. Contact them at 57 North Dale Street, St. Paul,
Minnesota 55102; (612) 224-5160.

9 | *Marital and Partner Investigations*

Signs of Infidelity

No one ever wants to think that a spouse or partner is cheating, but there are times when there are just too many clues to ignore the possibility. If you suspect your partner is cheating, here are some questions to ask yourself:

1. Does he or she have a hobby that takes them out of the house at least one or two nights a week? Is this a new hobby?
2. Does he or she have a new part-time job but no appreciable increase in income?
3. Does he or she go places where you cannot reach them?
4. Has there been a recent change in the way he or she looks, grooms themselves, or dresses?
5. Is he or she avoiding you in bed?
6. Is he or she suddenly wearing a new piece of jewelry or carrying a personal item that you didn't buy or know anything about?
7. Is he or she suddenly making more business trips, becoming harder to reach on trips, required to work considerably more nights and weekends?
8. Have you found condoms, birth control pills, or some other form of birth control that the two of you do not use together?

A few "yes" answers does not mean your partner is cheating. You'll notice most of the questions focus on recent changes. If your husband has always gone bowling on Tuesday nights, there is no reason to think he is doing anything but bowling now on Tuesday nights. Or if he has recently started to bowl and talks your ears off every Wednesday morning about the details of the game, it's a pretty good bet that's really where he was.

The time to worry is when a lot of these changes coincide with each other and there is no reasonable way to account for them. (And anytime the answer to Number 8 is yes, it's probably past time for worrying and time for some major action.) Interestingly enough, in some 80 to 90 percent of these cases, I and other private investigators have found that the client's fears are unfounded.

I've had several men come to me because they thought their girlfriends might be hookers; none has ever turned out to be a hooker. (One man was suspicious purely on his observation that her voice sounded "sexier and more professional" on her answering machine than in person. Case outcome: The girlfriend has a sexy, professional phone voice, but was not a prostitute.) In another case, a woman came to us because she thought her fiancé might be cheating on her. It turned out he was working at a part-time job to save money for her engagement ring.

As AIDS becomes more and more prevalent, we are getting more and more clients who want to make sure their partner is faithful. They also often want thorough background checks, especially in cases where they know or suspect drug use or a bisexual background.

As an investigator, I find marital and partner investigations extremely emotionally draining. So much of. people's lives are invested in the outcome. And telling a client that yes, his wife really was with another man this weekend or yes, we did see her boyfriend leave a well-known gay bar with another man is not easy. This is a very difficult kind of investigation to do completely on your own—not so much because you can't get the information, but because it becomes difficult to withhold growing doubts until information is certain.

Information for these cases is usually fairly easy to obtain. If the two people involved are married or live together, ofter it's just a matter of the suspicious party taking credit card and phone records out of the drawer or the trash can. Any records that aren't on the premises can easily be requested by a spouse. Also in these cases you already have some of the basic information, such as birth date and Social Security number, that you will need to check other public records.

But you can't usually prove infidelity with a paper trail: it may require surveillance, which is best done by a professional. Here are some examples of real cases that involved a combination of paper information gathering and surveillance. Also see Chapter 10, "Background Investigations," for more information on how to do background searches.

The Changeable Lawyer

Nancy came to us with an unusual complaint. Her fiancé, Michael, was too perfect. He was good-looking, considerate, a financially well-off lawyer who worked long, but not impossible hours. She had met him in a bar, and although she had since met many of his friends, she felt nervous because she didn't know anyone else who knew him very well. Her last relationship, which she had thought was leading to marriage, had ended when her boyfriend confessed that he had cheated on her. She had had no idea that he was cheating. This time, she wanted to be sure. She also wanted to be sure that Michael really was who he said he was—a lawyer, from a small town in the Northeast, etc.

We asked for, and she was able to supply, his birth date, Social Security number, address, phone number, place of work, work phone number, photograph, and other vital statistics. Then we got down to work, starting with confirming that he was who he said he was.

Board of Elections records confirmed his name and address were correct; motor vehicle records showed the same. We knew he was supposed to own his condo apartment—public records confirmed ownership. Records from the Bar Association showed he was indeed entitled to practice law in New York State. A call to the main switchboard of his company indicated he was employed there. Nothing unusual. He appeared to be who he said he was.

Randomly timed phone calls to his direct office line when he was supposed to be working late were always answered promptly by him. We obtained, from a contact with the company, a copy of the last two months of his American Express bill and checked it with Nancy. Almost all of the restaurants were places she had been with him on the dates indicated.

Meanwhile, we were also watching Michael. An investigator watched his home and his office. We could have set up electronic surveillance systems, but we didn't feel it was necessary unless something happened that would indicate the need for more sophisticated surveillance. Nothing unusual happened at Michael's office or home until the third night.

That night, after Michael had been home for about an hour, a very tall woman with too much make-up and flamboyant clothing left the building. Upon closer inspection, the investigator realized it was really Michael, but in drag! He followed him to a bar, where Michael had two drinks and then returned home. We immediately told

Nancy what we had seen, and she asked us to keep watching him. Two more times the scenario repeated itself. Michael did not leave the bar with anyone, but we couldn't be sure whether he was hitting a run of bad luck or if going to the bar was always the extent of his activities.

We sent someone into the bar to get more information. From conversations with the bartender, other patrons, and with Michael himself, it appeared that Michael liked to get dressed up, come out and socialize for a while, and then return home. In the meantime, at Nancy's request, we used a contact to check Michael's medical records. We found the results of past HIV tests were consistently negative. There were no indications of any other sexually transmitted diseases.

We again consulted with Nancy, being certain that she understood that just because we hadn't yet seen him with another man (or woman), we couldn't be certain that it would never happen. At this point, Nancy decided to take matters into her own hands and confronted Michael with what she knew. He readily confessed, swearing that he was never sexually involved with other people. Interestingly, Nancy decided to marry him after all, reasoning that he could easily have worse faults.

Playing Doctor

Owen came to us when he suspected Debbie, his wife of eight years, was cheating on him. Owen was the owner of a successful business and extremely wealthy. His wife had recently taken an inordinate interest in both golf and tennis, despite never having been sports oriented before. She had joined a local country club, where she spent many hours a day.

Owen had also found several pieces of sexy lingerie in her drawer. He hadn't bought them for her, and she had never worn them for him. At about the same time, Owen noticed that Debbie seemed to be very friendly with the physician who was treating his father for stomach cancer. As Debbie had always been close to her father-in-law, it wasn't unusual for her to accompany him to the doctor. On the occasions when Owen was also present, he thought she and the doctor seemed a little too friendly.

While all of this made Owen suspicious, it wasn't until she proposed attending a golf tournament in California that he really became worried. Debbie often traveled without him but not usually so far or for so long. He had also noticed that she had picked a time when business obligations made it impossible for him to join her. Her account of the trip when she returned didn't sound right. After agonizing for more than a week, he finally called us.

The first thing we did was to contact the doctor's office to find out if he had been out of town the previous week. Using a fictitious name, an investigator told the receptionist he had been in the office the last week and forgot to record the amount of the check he had paid with. Could she check it for him? She immediately told him that the doctor had been out of town the previous week, was it maybe the week before that he had been in the office? The investigator then pretended that he had called the wrong doctor and got off the phone, gracefully joking about his lack of memory these days.

Through a confidential contact, we then obtained the doctor's American Express bill, and got Debbie's bill from her husband. The statements showed that they had stayed at the same hotel, on the same dates, although in different rooms. The room numbers showed that the rooms were adjacent. The doctor's bill also showed large sums for dinner all three nights they were away (large enough for two people); Debbie's bill did not show any evening meals.

I then asked Owen to obtain copies of his phone bill for

the past three months, including local calls. The phone company doesn't particularly like to give out this information, but it will do so at the customer's request. The bills indicated daily (sometimes several times a day) calls from Owen's home to the doctor's office and home.

After this, the client asked us to set up surveillance at the doctor's home, which was located in an exclusive residential community in New Jersey. Because of the exclusivity of the area, we couldn't take the chance of having anyone "staked out" right outside of his home. Instead, we set up a video camera with a telescopic zoom lens in the taillight of a car that we parked nearby. The camera was hooked up to a video cassette recorder and microwave radio relay that our investigators could monitor from a less suspicious location about a half mile away from the home.

The investigators had been watching for about two hours when they saw Debbie's car pull into the doctor's driveway. After a few hours, she was seen leaving the house. Both events were captured on the video recorder, including the way Debbie was dressed. We continued surveillance for four more days, videotaping Debbie entering and leaving the house several times. The recorder had a time and date generator, which records and allows the viewer to see the date and time on the screen—and also allows the tape to be used as evidence if necessary.

We passed on to Owen the information that we had, and he requested that we follow Debbie on another trip she was making, this time to Florida. We obtained information from her American Express card again and saw that she had made advance reservations at a particular hotel. The doctor again had a separate room, but this time we were able to photograph the two holding hands and generally looking like they were having an affair.

A generous gratuity to the hotel manager got us copies of their registration cards, evidence that they had stayed in adjacent rooms. We continued to follow the two, noting that over the course of the next few days they went to several government buildings.

We did a search of the local public records and found that the doctor was applying for permits to build a medical facility in that township. He was also changing his voter's registration to that area. We then checked further and discovered the doctor had listed his New Jersey practice for sale in several medical publications. We also found that Debbie had changed her motor vehicle records and voter's registration to that township.

When we informed Owen, he immediately had his wife served with divorce papers and froze all their joint assets, preventing her from selling any property owned jointly through their marriage. Owen then confronted Debbie with the information he had. Because she was from a well-known family and anxious to avoid scandal, she agreed to a divorce settlement granting her far less than she ordinarily would have requested.

After the investigation, we were able to estimate that Owen had saved some $10 million in the divorce settlement by having the information we provided from our investigation!

10 | *Background Investigations*

There are all different kinds of background investigations. Sometimes they are personal—seeing if a boyfriend or girlfriend really is the person they claimed to be or trying to find out if a problematic neighbor or tenant has a history of making trouble. Or, at other times, they can be business-related: either involving standard background checks on potential employees or verifying information supplied by another company before purchasing or entering into business agreements with the company (generally called "due diligence").

As in most investigations, public records are the natural starting place. From these, you can generally find out any kind of criminal background, divorces, driving infractions, credit information (if the person authorizes you to do the check), and financial problems, among other things. Sometimes surveillance and other contacts are needed. Sometimes everything you need is right there in the public records. Here are some examples of the various kinds of investigations, showing how each step logically flows from the previous one.

Head Games

It's a sign of the times, but more and more these days, we get cases involving a person who wants to do a background check on a girlfriend or boyfriend. People who meet in bars, at singles weekends, through the personals, even at work often come to the realization that they don't really know anything about the other person besides what they've been told by that person. They *want* to trust the other person, but....Parents, too, are often concerned, and usually don't want a son or daughter to know about it. In these cases, the girlfriend, boyfriend, or parents usually come to us quietly, sometimes somewhat embarrassed, but determined to know the truth.

Many times the person is exactly who they claimed to be. But there are exceptions. For example: Sharon Buchbinder was thirty, single, a lawyer, healthy, and attractive. When she had met Bart Winfield at a singles weekend, there was an immediate chemistry between the two. Bart was a psychiatrist, thirty-three, apparently well off, with an office in his apartment.

The two had started dating and after several weeks Bart had asked Sharon to invest some money—$25,000—in a medical center he was trying to put together in a lower-income area. Because of the double connection—love and money—Sharon wanted to be sure that Bart was who he claimed to be.

She was able to supply us with basic information about him: name, address, phone number, birth date, the medical school he had attended, and more. We started with the Department of Motor Vehicles and found that his Mercedes was registered in his name at the address we already had. However, a further search showed that Bart didn't own the car, he was merely leasing it. Not a great sign, but also not terrible. People lease for many reasons.

The trouble really started when we checked with Professional Licensing and found that Bart was not licensed. Then we checked with the medical school from which he supposedly had received his degree. By this time it was no surprise to find out there was no degree and no attendance at the school, ever. We reported back to Sharon, who wanted more information. She was considering prosecuting him, but knew she would need more before she could proceed.

We went back to the public records and did a full search in the county he lived in. We found no record of any judgments, lawsuits, or police involvement. We moved onto a "history search" of motor vehicle records to try to find out more about his past. This showed that he had previously owned several vehicles at a different address, in a different county.

We checked the local public records in that county and found Bart had owned property in that county—with a woman named Michelle Locker. The house had been sold at foreclosure; in that county we also found several judgments against him—personally and against some companies he had been involved with.

When we got the business certificates for the companies, it turned out that he had owned two different psychotherapy practices. We checked the records on those companies and found both of them had been closed due to lawsuits and complaints against him and his companies. Conversations with several of the complainants—attractive young women—revealed that he had conned money from them for business purposes that never materialized.

Then we ran a criminal conviction search. No surprises here either: convictions for fraud, practicing without a license, larceny, assault, and passing bad checks. One of the assault complainants turned out to be an ex-girlfriend who had asked for her money back. He had never served any jail time, just received fines, suspended sentences, and probation.

At this point there was just one last thing to check. Who was Michelle Locker? Since they had lived at the same address, we took a chance and checked the divorce records of the State Supreme Court and there it was: the docket number for the divorce filed by Michelle Locker. Going a step further, we also found a judgment against him for nonsupport by Michelle Locker.

When we gave the entire report to Sharon, she asked us to take the matter to the police. But, technically, no new crime had yet been committed. He had a past and he had lied to Sharon, but Sharon hadn't given him any money for the medical center. Yet, that is. She was ready for revenge now, and she knew how to get it.

At her request, we set up a hidden camera with a time and date generator in her living room. Bart asked her for the $25,000 for his center, and she gave him a check, asking him not to deposit it for three days until she was sure the money was in her account. When she asked for a promissory note, she received one signed by Bart, on behalf of the clinic. Since there was no clinic, the note was fraudulent; if he had simply signed in his own name, we might have had a problem prosecuting.

The tape of the conversation (legal in this case because Sharon was a party to the conversation and had consented to its recording; see Chapter 6 for more information on audio and video taping) and the check given to Bart were enough for the District Attorney to get an indictment and conviction. In the process, Sharon got a broken heart, but it wasn't as bad as it would have been later. And she saved herself $25,000.

The Nuisance Neighbor

You know who I mean: the ones who play the stereo at full volume until 4:00 A.M., or let the pit-bull terrier roam freely around the neighborhood, or have a constant stream of scary looking "friends" in and out of the place. These are fairly common and straightforward cases for private investigators, sometimes initiated by the landlord, more often by the neighbors who are just plain fed up. They are also fairly easy to follow up yourself, if you are not willing to spend money for what most of us consider the basic right to live in peace.

The nature of the problem you're having with a neighbor will point you in the direction of what kinds of past problems to look for. For instance, if you suspect your neighbor is involved with drugs in any way or has a serious alcohol problem, you will want to check with the Department of Motor Vehicles for any violations and check court records for convictions of any crimes. Noisy, nuisance, or just plain nasty neighbors might also have court records; or you might learn more from a previous landlord or neighbor.

What you find out through any of these searches might be enough to help you legally to get rid of troublesome neighbors. Even if that's not the case, if the background is problematic, there's a good chance they will voluntarily change their ways when they know that you know—and are willing to tell others whom they might not want told. Here's a sample involving a woman who ended up being more trouble than anyone initially anticipated.

Our investigation started when a client, Stephen Kane, asked us to conduct a search on a woman who lived directly above him in an apartment building in Flushing, New York. Ms. E. Smith had recently moved into the building and was consistently blasting her stereo late at night, and she had all kinds of people constantly coming in and out of her apartment.

Stephen had tried to speak to her pleasantly but had only received nasty and rude responses. He had also contacted his landlord, but the landlord was reluctant to do anything, possibly fearing that he might be held accountable for allowing her to move in.

We had a hard time at the beginning of the investigation

because we couldn't track down the usual public records: There was no telephone listing for her in the building, no Board of Elections records, and we couldn't do a motor vehicle search because we didn't even have her first name yet, much less her birth date. The landlord could have supplied the full name, as well as other information from the lease, but he was not cooperating.

Finally, through a pretext, we were able to get some information from her utility service, including the date her gas and electricity were started and—more importantly—her full name (Elayne Smith) and her unlisted telephone number. Now we were in business. We were able to do the motor vehicle search, which gave us her previous address—and a host of driving infractions, including numerous suspensions for Driving While Intoxicated (DWI) and Driving Under the Influence (DUI), several accidents, and a suspension of her vehicle registration because of a lapse in her car insurance.

From there, a check with the Parking Violations Bureau told us she owed more than $2,000 in outstanding tickets unpaid on the vehicle previously registered to her. A further search of the public records showed a judgment by her previous landlord for $6,000 in back rent and damages to her apartment.

Time to speak directly with the previous landlord. Because of all the money she owed him and problems that she had caused for him, he was more than willing to supply information about her. He told us she was a "crazy lady" who acted irrationally most of the time. She had destroyed parts of that apartment and had actually been evicted by the city Marshal.

Then the landlord had gone to court for back rent and damages, and another tenant in the building had filed a criminal complaint against her. Knowing that, we did a criminal record search and found that she had been convicted of criminal harassment against one of the other building tenants. She had received a suspended sentence and a fine.

We had all the records certified and passed them on to Stephen Kane, who gave them to the landlord. At that point, the landlord had no choice but to notify the building manager and custodial staff of the probability of a problem. Eventually, Ms. Smith did cause more problems in this building, and she was finally evicted. Unfortunately, our client had to spend his own money to get rid of a problem that he shouldn't have had to deal with in the first place. Had the landlord done some or all of these checks on his own before renting Ms. Smith the apartment, he could have saved considerable time, energy, and money for everyone.

The Local Drug Dealer

Proving that a neighbor is dealing drugs is sometimes difficult, even with the techniques of private investigators, such as surveillance that includes still and video photography. Individuals and private investigators can't actually buy the drugs to prove drug dealing, but you can try to get enough evidence to establish probable cause and then hand it over to the police.

An alternative is to try to get rid of the person on some other grounds, such as increased foot traffic in the building or neighborhood, noise, litter, vandalism, vagrancy, and other associated problems. If public records indicate past problems, especially arrests or criminal convictions, you can certainly use them to make your case stronger.

Even if you try to have someone evicted for a cause other than drugs, if drugs are part of the problem, there are subtle ways to let a judge know that. For example, if you present photos of the litter created by the tenant, make sure that they prominently feature any drug-related paraphernalia such as syringes or rolling papers. Bring as much evidence as possible to court, including photos, recordings, and video, if possible.

It's often easier to get other neighbors to testify against a drug dealer about noise, vandalism, etc. than about the actual drugs. There's also a good chance that just the service of the summons will be enough to get rid of a person who can't take the risk of standing trial.

Employee Background Checks

Since 1987, when it became illegal to use lie detectors (polygraphs) in the hiring process, careful employee background checks have become more and more common. Most of these can be easily performed by the personnel department or hiring supervisor, as well as by a private investigator employed specifically to perform such checks. From a typical employment application, you already have much of the basic information about the applicant: name, address, date of birth, Social Security number, and permission to obtain a credit report.

As in any other area of life, if a person's resume appears too good to be true, it probably is! Here's a classic example. A company hired us to check the background of a job applicant who seemed perfect. David Gales had a degree from a top college and references from prestigious companies, yet he was asking for about $15,000 less than the job would normally pay. In such cases, a background check usually includes fairly standard stuff: references, credit history, motor vehicles, and criminal checks. For the record, under the "Fair Credit Reporting Act," it's legal to check credit history when the person gives you permission.

The check was routine enough to begin with: three credit cards, all paid on time, one car loan for a fairly expensive car, an apparently clean criminal record. Then we found what might or might not have been a problem: His driving record indicated one DWI and one DUI. Not horrible, but an indication of a possible drinking problem.

The next move was to check his business references. We started with the names of the supervisors that he had listed from his two previous companies. Not surprisingly, they both said he was a good worker, reliable, punctual, etc. References supplied by a potential employee are almost not worth checking: People don't list anyone whom they think won't give them a good reference. So we took the reference check a step farther and found out the name of the manager of his previous division, who had not been listed as a reference.

We were told that Gales had been an assistant researcher, not a full researcher as he had stated on his resume. The manager didn't know exactly what his salary had been, but was able to confirm that it was considerably less than Gales had stated. He also implied, although he didn't come out and say it, that Gales's performance had not really been satisfactory. (In today's litigious society, many are afraid to give anything but a good reference for fear of being slapped with a lawsuit. Anyone doing a reference check should always be prepared to read between the lines of a conversation to discern if the reference-giver is truly giving a good reference or just being cautious.) We had a similar experience when we checked references (both the name Gales supplied and the direct supervisor) with the second company listed.

The next step was back to the public records, and here's where it really got interesting: A criminal search in the county where he had received his DWI and DUI showed he had been convicted of three robberies! It turned out all three of the complainants had been *previous employers*. Then we checked his educational records and found they, too, had been falsified—he hadn't received a degree as stated, but merely attended the institution for one semester. Needless to say, the company did not hire him.

Business Background Investigations

Before entering into any kind of business arrangement, it's wise to check the veracity of what the company has told you. The days of sealing a business deal with a handshake are long gone, as are the days when you could believe what someone told you simply on the person's word (although truth be told, you never could).

The most seemingly innocent, honest companies can actually be involved in all sorts of sordid affairs. On the other hand, just because a business owner might appear to be of somewhat dicey character doesn't mean the business itself is. The only way to know for sure is to do your homework.

In fact, checks that appear to be purely routine sometimes end up leading off in completely unanticipated directions, as happened in the following case. A manufacturer, Diamond Industries, contacted us before purchasing the Pizzero Trucking Company.

In thirty years, Diamond Co. had grown from a two-man operation to a company with several hundred employees. At the time, it was cash poor but asset rich in manufacturing equipment, had an excellent client base, a large accounts receivable, a desirable industrial property, and a large amount of new manufacturing equipment.

Pizzero was a relatively new company that had grown rapidly in the past five years. They were cash rich, had many trucks, and were looking to expand. For the past three years, the two companies had worked together with no problems.

Diamond Company was considering purchasing Pizzero and asked us to do a fairly routine check on the company and its ownership before entering into any agreement. On the surface, everything appeared to be fine, but Diamond had some reservations. Specifically, they wanted to make sure that the company was doing as well as it appeared to be and that their money was legitimate. In other words, that it wasn't mob connected.

Since the sale was already in the discussion stages, Diamond had a lot of the paperwork on Pizzero in its possession. They passed on to us all the information they had, and then we went to work. Since we knew the address of the company, we checked Cole's Directory to see what other companies might be located at that address. The search revealed several other companies in that industrial complex.

Among them was a company called CLT Ltd., whose name came up again when we searched for lien information. We found records of several liens involving Pizzero and the purchase of CLT. The liens covered property such as all the debtors' rights, titles, and interest to the trucking routes, stops, and customer lists to be sold to the debtor—in other words, Pizzero had bought out CLT. Then we found a financial statement regarding a loan to Pizzero; the bank had put a lien on all personal property, fixtures of the debtors, and so on.

A further investigation revealed that Pizzero had sold its accounts receivable to the bank, a kind of loan called "factoring." The bank would receive payment that would normally go to Pizzero and deduct the amount of the money they were owed by the company plus interest—which generally works out to an exorbitantly high service fee. Other investigations showed Pizzero and CLT owed considerable taxes.

A federal record search showed nothing out of the ordinary, no judgments or liens against the companies in Federal Court. We did, however, find judgments against Bill

Pizzero, the president of the company.

Further searches about Mr. Pizzero revealed he had a substantial mortgage on his house that had been paid off rapidly within the past few months. A motor vehicle search showed he had recently purchased an expensive car—all in cash. When we checked the local records in Mr. Pizzero's county, we found a judgment against him regarding a business transaction in which he had pledged stocks of his company as collateral.

At this point, we gave a preliminary report to our client. He thought, and we agreed, that the circumstances were suspicious enough to warrant a check of any criminal record history of Mr. Pizzero's. After doing this search, we found he had been arrested and convicted of fraud regarding another business he had been involved in a few years back.

By now, it was clear something fishy was going on. With our client's permission, we decided to see if the Organizod Crime Task Force had any information on Mr. Pizzero. In certain situations, private investigators and government agencies will share information. Since we had uncovered a possible fraudulent conveyance of business assets, and what my client believed was an attempted scam, we had information to give the Feds.

In return, we learned that the Organized Crime Task Force was actively investigating the principals who had started the trucking company a few years ago. It was laundering illegally obtained money through the corporation, developing credit lines and good business references, and purchasing equipment on credit. The company's sole reason to exist was to build up the business, sell off the assets, and pocket whatever money it could.

We presented all the information to our client. With this information in hand, he knew he would be taking on tremendous liabilities that had not been disclosed if he went ahead with the purchase of the company. He waited until the meeting right before the closing of the sale to present the report to the sellers and their attorneys. Of course, at that time, he also told them he would not be purchasing Pizzero Trucking Company.

The story didn't end there, though. Another company wasn't as smart as Diamond. They didn't do the proper background check and went ahead and purchased Pizzero Trucking Company. I found out about it when I read the story in the newspaper: Pizzero Trucking Company and all its officers had been indicted on a charge of Racketeer Influenced Corruption (the RICO Act). The purchasing company had gone to the Attorney General's office after finding out it had been ripped off.

It turned out that Pizzero's owners were part of one of the largest crime families in New York City. They were using the company to launder money and as a front for illegal union activities. They were also using the trucks to transport stolen goods across state lines, even on occasion hijacking one of their own trucks for the insurance. The background investigation we did on behalf of Diamond, which prevented its purchase of Pizzero, was worth its weight in, well...diamonds!

11 | *Property Investigations*

Another category of background investigation is called property investigation. For example, some tenants may be more than just a bother or a nuisance; the landlord might feel that it's necessary or desirable to obtain some in-depth information about a particular tenant. With commercial property, for instance, the landlord might be concerned about the kind of business being conducted on the premises. Another big concern, particularly in cities with limited or expensive housing, is illegal subletting for profit (profit for the person doing the subletting, that is, not profit for the landlord) and using commercial spaces for residential purposes. In some of these instances, public records can provide much of the evidence you'll need; in others, some subterfuge or surveillance is usually called for.

A Tricky Business

What do you do if you suspect that the masseuse to whom you've rented the third floor does a little more than massage behind closed doors? Or that the health club on the street level of your building is more interested in exercising certain parts of the body than others? Your first step is to check the public records to see if the stated purpose of the business is the kind that is generally licensed. In the case of a health club, for instance, you would check to see if the health club has a license. If there's no license, you are off to a good start—you can evict on that alone. Even if there is a license, make sure that the names on the license are the same as those on the lease itself.

Assuming that everything does check out, but you are still suspicious, there are two ways to go. You can keep checking public records in the hopes of coming up with violations of the business or the people who own the business. (See Chapter 10, "Background Investigations," for more information.) Or you can send someone in to get more information through questioning, surveillance, recording, and whatever other means might be necessary. Just remember that if you want to bring a case to court, you're going to have to obtain your information in legal ways that can be used in court. If you suspect illegal sexual activity, check local newspapers to see if the address is advertised or listed.

If you suspect the premises is being used for illegal gambling, such as a numbers drop, be careful about how you proceed. In some places, it's the landlord who will be held accountable, not the person who's renting the space. In other words, if you go straight to the police without any evidence, you could end up getting *yourself* a summons! Again, consider sending someone in undercover to see what's really going on. Have the person buy a number if possible; usually the bookie will give a slip to the purchaser, which can then be used as evidence.

Commercial Spaces as Residences

Sometimes lofts or other large commercial spaces are rented and then illegally subdivided and rented to other individuals. If you suspect this is happening, there are a few ways to confirm it. One is to check the utility records to see if water and electricity use are substantially higher than for other comparable properties. Another is to check telephone records for the number of telephone numbers at a particular address. Also be sure to check whose name they are in. It is not inconceivable that a business or even an individual has more than one phone number, but in legitimate cases all the numbers should be in the name of the person you're renting to or in a legitimate business name.

You can also try having a friendly chat with the mail carrier for the building. There's no guarantee, but he or she might be willing to tell you the names of the people getting mail at that address. Once you know the names to check, you can obtain legal confirmation of each name from the Post Office through the Freedom of Information Act. Be aware, though, that some illegal subletters are pretty savvy--they know to get their mail delivered to a P. O. Box rather than the street address.

Another possibility is to send someone in undercover to try to rent space there. Of course, before this is tried, a fair amount of background checking will be necessary to know what the setup is. Your official tenant *will* be suspicious if someone just knocks on the door out of the blue and asks to sublet a room or apartment illegally! If the person is successful, they should be certain to get some sort of written receipt and should consider video and/or audio taping any conversations as evidence.

Illegal Tenancy

This kind of problem is most common in large cities with rent regulation and rent control laws. (New York City, for example, is notorious for it.) Illegal subletting involves one person's legally renting an apartment or house, and in turn, subletting that property to another person, generally for a substantial profit. The profit motive comes in the disparity between the amount the legal tenant actually has to pay for rent and the *perceived value* of the property.

For example, a person who has been living in an apartment for ten years might be paying $350 a month in rent. Meanwhile, other, comparable apartments in the same building might be going for $800 a month. The legal tenant sublets the apartment to someone else and pockets the $450 difference. A good deal for the tenant; a loss of $450 a month for the landlord. Even if regulation prevents the landlord from renting the apartment for the full $800 market value, there would still be a substantial increase in rent with the change in tenancy.

Besides the monthly loss of income for the landlord, there can be a major difference in selling price if the landlord decides to convert the building to co-ops. In some instances, the difference in the selling price of an occupied unit versus an unoccupied unit (which the apartment would be if the landlord can prove illegal subletting) can be as much as $100,000!

So how do you prove illegal subletting? First, you need to know the rules of the game; in other words, you need to know exactly what illegal act it is that you are trying to prove. In New York City, for example, a rent-regulated apartment can only be retained under certain conditions: The tenant must live in the apartment at least half the year, or if absent longer, be able to demonstrate an intention to return; subletting for certain periods of time is legal (generally for two out of four years); and the rent charged to a sublessee cannot be more than the landlord could legally charge for the same apartment. Most of the proof revolves around public records that can show the person who claims to be living in the apartment really lives elsewhere.

Such proof can usually be found in the form of voter registration records, driver's licenses, car registrations, credit card and bank statements, telephone records, and court papers. If necessary, personal or electronic surveillance can also be conducted (it's easy enough to, say, install a video camera behind the wall in the lobby of a building as long as you have the landlord's permission). In many cases, it's never even necessary to go to court. Once you can show the person who holds the lease that you have proof of illegal activities, you may see some quick action.

For example, my company was once hired to confirm the status of several rent-regulated apartments in a fashionable building in one of New York City's better neighborhoods. The apartments were leased by six executives from a large advertising agency, who collectively controlled several apartments that they used to put up corporate guests.

Careful inspection of public records and work with some confidential contacts showed us that all six earned very generous salaries and owned their own homes. A few weeks of surveillance showed that none used the apartments as a primary residence. We never had to go to court. All we did was show the executives some pictures we had taken of their houses and made it clear we were prepared to go to court if necessary. They quickly gave up their leases.

Another typical problem landlords have is with people who claim to have rights to an apartment through "succession" laws, which allow any relative to take over a rent-regulated apartment after the primary lease holder dies— provided that the relative has been living there, too. Not surprisingly, when the tenant of a low-rent apartment dies, there is often at least one person who claims to have been living with that relative all along. Proof of other residency can again lie in the public records, particularly Board of Elections and motor vehicle records, as well as bank accounts, property deeds, insurance statements, and anything else that typically lists a home address.

Landlords will often already have a wealth of legally obtained information about their tenants, including their Social Security number and permission to run a credit check, which makes checking public records that much easier, at least to start. If you are trying to confirm that someone does not really live where the person claims to live, also be aware of where a rent check is issued from: Does the check for an apartment on New York's Fifth Avenue have a printed address of San Diego, California? Or did it come in an envelope with a postmark from another city? You don't usually need to hire a private investigator to get to the bottom of this kind of problem.

12 | *Genealogical Searches*

One of the most personally rewarding kinds of searches can be the quest for your own family's history. Since Alex Haley's groundbreaking novel, *Roots*, more Americans than ever have taken up the search for their forebears.

Like any other search, tracking down your family history is a combination of pulling together data from public records and information gleaned from other sources, such as talks with relatives, old family Bibles, diaries, and letters. Finding out your family's history can be fascinating, fulfilling, sometimes even heartbreaking.

There are whole books dedicated to this engrossing topic, but here are the basics.

Family Name

Before you do anything else, write down your family name and any other variations of that name. Why? Because there's more than a good chance that your family's name has been changed one or more times along the way. Ellis Island officials might have changed the name slightly (or completely), your own ancestors might have "Americanized" the name, or, although difficult to conceive of now, they might have spelled their own name different ways at different times. (Daniel Boone was also known to sign his name Bone and Boon!) If you're prepared ahead of time, it's less likely that you will miss or ignore one of the changes when you come across it.

Start with all the ways that your name can be spelled and still likely be pronounced the same way. (Burke could also be Berke, Burk, or thirty-four other variations.) Then move on to other names that are pronounced similarly to the way yours is (here Burke might become Bark, Bork, Beerk, and so on). The easiest way to do this part is just to think of all the ways strangers mispronounce your name.

Start With Yourself

You probably already know more about your family than you realize. While it's up to you to decide exactly how much you want to know about each ancestor, most people start with the basics: name; date and place of birth; date and place of marriage and to whom; name, date, and place of birth of any children (and their marriages, etc.); date, place, and cause of death. Other favorites include profession, military history, religion, immigration from where, and why, if applicable. See how far back you can go right now using only your memory.

Interview Relatives

You might think you have already heard all your Great-aunt Agnes's stories, but interview her anyway. Chances are she has a few tales tucked away—and they just might be the most juicy ones! When possible, talk with relatives in person. Tape record all conversations—you *will* forget the details if you don't. If you are interviewing someone you're particularly close to, consider videotaping the conversation for a permanent memory.

If you can't get to someone in person, speak with them on the telephone (again tape recording, but be sure to get permission) or write a letter. If you go the letter route, don't just ask for anything that can be remembered. Ask as many specific questions as you can think of to prompt memories, and then ask that they add anything else they can think of.

When it comes to older relatives—do it now! It's not morbid, simply a fact, that people don't live forever. And when they are gone, so are their memories.

Family Memorabilia

You might already have a wealth of information in your own attic or basement. When visiting older relatives, in particular, ask if you can look through their old keepsakes. While you probably won't be able to take anything with you, looking through the memorabilia can give you some great insights into your family history. Here are some things to look for.

• *Personal records* include family photo albums, scrapbooks, diaries, Bibles, letters, yearbooks, autograph albums, baby books, newspaper clippings, diplomas, awards, employment files, hospitalization records, doctor bills, marriage certificates from religious ceremonies, and so on. You might also come across clothing, books, jewelry, furniture—items that won't necessarily give you any facts but can give you clues about the personality and tastes of the people who owned them.

• *Legal and government papers* include birth certificates, death certificates, wills, deeds, mortgages, contracts, tax records, military discharge papers and awards, passports, citizenship or naturalization papers, Social Security cards, etc. Many of these are also public records, but why go through the hassle of looking for them when you might already have copies?

The Game Plan

At this point, you probably want to know everything

about everyone whose name you have come across so far. Don't worry, you probably will eventually. But not yet. Trying simultaneously to track every family line you come across will result in massive confusion. Decide on the first family line that you want to trace—usually the family surname or the mother's maiden name.

Every step back in time will give you more names to work with, more options to choose from. As a general rule, it's best to stick with one line at a time; if you get stuck on any one line, drop it for a while and move on to another.

Genealogical Libraries

Before you go any further, now's the time to see if other people have already done some of your work for you. If it's been done, the most likely place to find it is at the *Family History Library of the Church of Latter Day Saints* (formerly called the Genealogical Library), the most comprehensive library for genealogical research. Based in Salt Lake City, Utah, the library boasts the world's largest, most complete collection of genealogical information.

Open to the public, the library was funded to gather records that help people—all people, not just Mormons—trace their family lines. The library is *not* intended to be used as a resource for tracing the living or the missing. A branch system has existed since 1964, with more than 11,000 branches, called Family History Centers, in the United States and throughout the world.

Services offered by the main library and its branches include a catalog of all the library's records; an International Genealogical Index with listings of more than 100 million births, christenings, and marriages; publications and classes on how to do a genealogical search; computerized databases of individuals and families interested in sharing information; and a list of accredited professional genealogical searchers.

The libraries house records gathered from around the world, including those pertaining to birth, death, marriage, the military, land, and probate. Other information includes U.S. Census data, passenger ship lists, church registers, naturalization records, and more.

For more information or to find out where the nearest local branch is, contact:

The Family History Library of the Church of Latter Day Saints
35 Northwest Temple Street
Salt Lake City, Utah 84150
(801) 240-2331

In addition to the Family History Library and centers, many public libraries also have extensive genealogical information available to the public. The New York City Public Library has one of the most extensive public library collections. If you know where your ancestors first entered the country, or where groups of them settled, try any large public library in that area for possible documentation about your family. Often, when you can't go to a particular library in person, the librarians will answer specific questions for you by mail.

During your search, don't forget state libraries (which sometimes have extensive information about the early history of the state and region) and local and national genealogical societies.

Public Records

These records are just as valuable for tracking historical information as they are for discovering information about a living person. Not only will any existing public records fill in holes about the specific person you are looking for, but many of them will provide information or clues that can take you even further back or in a different direction. In addition, these records can confirm—or perhaps disprove—information you've gleaned in other ways. In many instances, they can also provide invaluable clues about the lifestyle, habits, concerns, and even thoughts of the people you're researching.

Local Records

If you know the town, city, or general area that an ancestor was born in or resided in for any period of time, start with the local courthouse and County Clerk's office. (See also Chapter 2 for more information on researching local records.)

What if you can't find the records where you think they are supposed to be? Does no marriage certificate for your great grandparents mean they really weren't married? No! It simply means public record keeping in the past was often a hit-or-miss affair. The lack of a public record for an event doesn't indicate that it didn't occur, simply that it wasn't publicly recorded by the government. It might, however, have been recorded and kept by religious officials. Religious institutions often keep records concerning membership, marriages, funerals, baptisms, and so on.

Here are some of the local records you will want to look for:

• *Birth Certificate:* provides the date, time, and place of birth, the sex of the baby, the name, and *names of the parents.* Let's say you have been able to trace your mother's family line only back to her parents. If you know your grandfather's name and his place of birth, his birth certificate will provide the names of his parents, allowing you to go a full generation further back.

• *Marriage Certificate:* provides the place and date of the marriage, residences of the man and woman, *the presiding official,* and *the woman's maiden name.* Since most marriages in the past were religious ceremonies, knowing who the presiding official was should tell you the religion of at least one of the spouses (you can't assume that just because your family is, say, Catholic now, that it always was). Perhaps the most important piece of information here is the woman's maiden name. Knowing that will allow you to look for her birth certificate, which will provide information about her parents and allow you to start looking for information about her other relatives.

In addition to the actual marriage certificate, *marriage bands,* or *bonds of intention,* were common in many places. Legal documents that proclaimed the marriage intent were posted by the suitor (often accompanied by financial penalties if he defaulted). Look for these documents in city and county records.

• *Death Certificate:* provides name, age, date and place of death, doctor's name, and *cause of death.* The latter, in addition to being merely interesting, can help you develop a family medical history. Such a history can show trends and illnesses that might someday prove invaluable to you and other living members of your family.

• *Other local public records* includes *wills, probate documents, land deeds, tax and voting lists,* and *commissioners' records* that show the location of roads. Early land records often indicate the time, place, and length of residence for transactions and might include information about other property or relatives. Wills, too, can supply invaluable information about property owned, other relatives, and the nature of their relationships: Why did Great-great Uncle Joe leave his house to a distant cousin instead of his son? How come Great Grandfather Isaac left three of his children money outright and put money for the fourth in a trust?

Federal Records

These records can supply a wealth of information about ancestors, such as who lived in a household, military records, where and when someone immigrated from another country, and more. Many of these records are kept in the National Archives, in Washington, D.C. and in several regional branches of the archives. For more information about the archives or to find out the location of the nearest branch, write to the National Archives and Records Administration at Pennsylvania Avenue N.W., Washington, D.C. 20408, or call (202) 501-5402. Here are some of the records you will find housed there:

• *United States Census Records:* The United States Census was started in 1790 and is taken every ten years; records are public from 1790 through 1910. After that, records are confidential by restrictions of the 1974 Privacy Act. While you cannot go through the records after 1910 yourself, you can, however, obtain some information about your relatives by writing to the Bureau of the Census, Pittsburg, Kansas 66762. After you fill out a form, for a fee researchers will send you the personal information from an ancestor's census records, such as age, place of birth, and citizenship.

In the first census, in 1790, only the male heads of families were actually *named*, although other males and females and slaves were counted. The 1850 census was the first to name each *free* person in a household and included information on address, age, sex, color, occupation, value of real estate owned, place of birth, and whether or not the person was married within the year. For each slave, there was a listing of age, sex, and color, but no name.

It wasn't until the 1870 census that blacks, Chinese, and

American Indians were listed by name. This census also shows the month of birth of all citizens within the year and the month of marriage, also within the year. In 1880, the census started to list the relationship of all family members to the head of the household and gave the *birthplace of the parents* of each person listed, a clue to the foreign birthplace of immigrant ancestors. The 1890 census was the first to include the *exact* birth date of everyone listed.

Be aware that the census is far from infallible. Just as many people today are still afraid that the information on a census form will come back to haunt them in some way, there was a time when the census takers were thought to be tax collectors in disguise, prompting many to give inaccurate information or to try to elude the census altogether. There was also a time when census takers were paid in proportion to the number of families they canvassed, which led to the invention of people. Finally, census takers then and now, as well as the people they canvassed, were as prone to innocent error as anybody else.

If you know the county and state where your ancestors lived, here's some of the information you might discover through the census:

1. Your ancestor's occupation
2. Immigration and domestic changes of residence
3. Property information
4. Changes in the number of people in the family from decade to decade
5. Who died when, and at what age
6. Marriage and remarriage information

When going through the census, keep an eye out for other people with the same name in the same general location. Families in the past tended to stay in the same area much more than they do today. Chances are another family with the same last name in the same town was a relative—

perhaps even parents, taking your search a step further back.

Also be aware of slight changes in spelling: Burke in 1890 might have been Berke in 1880. The family might have changed the spelling itself—or the census taker might just have been careless.

• *Military Records:* Many of the Revolutionary War records were destroyed in fires, but some still exist. The National Archives has old military records, including both Union and Confederate veterans. These records generally list rank, age, place of enlistment, and other details of service.

• *Pensions and Bounty Land Grants:* Granted after military service, records pertaining to pensions and bounty land grants can hold a wealth of information. The applications usually show name, rank, military unit, place of residence, and often a detailed explanation of battlefield service. The files also often contain material needed to justify veterans' claims to these grants, which can be anything from an affidavit from a relative to whole pages torn from family Bibles.

• *Ships' Passenger Lists:* These records can be extremely helpful in determining when and where ancestors came from, but be aware that there are huge gaps in both the lists and the information on the lists. Original lists were prepared on board the ship by the captain and then filed when the ship reached port. If you're lucky, they will contain information about the name of the vessel, master, and port of embarkation; date and port of arrival; passenger name, sex, age, and occupation, as well as the country (or countries) of origin. The National Archives will do the search for you if you can provide the name and the approximate date and port of arrival (the vessel's name is helpful too).

• *Naturalization Petition:* With the information you obtain from ships' passenger lists (or any other means), you can write to the Immigration and Naturalization Service (119 D Street, N.W., Washington, D.C. 20536) or call (202) 514-2000, for a copy of your ancestor's naturalization petition, which should include birthplace and parents' names.

Foreign Records

If you have worked hard and been lucky, you might be able to trace some or all of your family lines back to the original arrival in this country. You might want to stop at this point or take the search further and try to get information about ancestors in other countries. Seeing the house where your great grandmother was born or meeting third cousins who still live in the "old country" can be one of the most rewarding parts of any search.

Before you take off for parts unknown, there's still some work to be done in the United States. The minimum information you should have at hand is your ancestor's name, the part of the country he or she came from, and an approximate time of departure from that place. Then head back to the Family History Library or one of its branches; it has large quantities of records from countries that have historically supplied the U.S. with immigrants.

If you decide to search for records in the country of origin, the procedure isn't all that different there than it is in the United States. To some degree or another, most countries keep much the same records: census, birth, death, marriage, military, tax, and so on. For more information about where and how to obtain records from a particular country of origin, contact that country's embassy in Washington, D.C., the American Embassy located in that country, or a local or national branch of any genealogical society.

Part III
Future Steps

13 | *Protecting Your Own Privacy*

Now that you know some of the things you can easily find out about other people, you might be wondering just how much of your own history is available to other people interested in you and your habits! It's virtually impossible to eliminate all traces of your history, but there are certain steps you can take to minimize other people's access to information that you consider private.

When it comes to public records, most of them are just that—public information. You can, however, control some of them:

- You can pay to have your phone number not listed (see below).
- You can pay to have your new address not accessible when you have your mail forwarded through the Post Office.
- At your request, your marriage records can be "sealed," in other words, closed to the public.
- Court records are generally public information, but if information comes up that you consider confidential—usually medical or financial data— you can request that the judge seal those portions of the record. Note that it's only a request, you can't enforce it.

There are also steps you can take to limit access to

information about you and to ensure that the information that is on record is at least correct. Here's how.

The Telephone

If you don't want other people to be able to easily find your phone number, it's simple enough to make sure the number is not listed. But, you have to pay for the privilege. (It's less trouble for the phone company to list your number along with everyone else's than to go to the bother of keeping it private.) Also be aware that there's often a difference between phone numbers that are "nonpublished" and those that are "not listed." A nonpublished number, as the name implies, is not put in the telephone book, but is obtainable simply by calling Information. A number that's not listed is not obtainable at all through regular channels with the phone company.

If your phone number is unlisted, you can also ask your company for a "red flag" noting when anyone calls to inquire about your phone number. A warning here, though. I've done this and then called the phone company pretending to be someone else asking for information about my own phone number. I didn't receive the information—but I was also never notified that anyone had tried to obtain it.

Of course, you can completely defeat the point of being not listed by including your phone number on all sorts of other forms, such as your voter registration card, or having it printed on your personal checks, or handwriting it in when you use a credit card. Most people are intimidated into giving out their phone number in such circumstances, but you don't have to be; simply say your phone number is unlisted and leave it at that.

Besides the question of listing your phone number, new technology is leading in ever more complicated areas when it comes to privacy protection. For instance, in many areas now, users can simply push a two-digit code to return any phone call. This "call-return" service will dial the number, but not actually let you know what the number is.

Services like this can be a double-edged sword: While you might appreciate your ability to use that service, there may be times when you make a phone call and don't want the person you're calling to be able to return your call. As always, as fast as someone comes up with a new technology, someone else comes up with a block for it. In the above case, you can pay for the "privilege" of not allowing others to return your calls through this service.

A similar option through many phone companies is "call tracing," by which a person can have crank phone calls traced by pushing a two-digit code. Again, you don't receive the phone number of the person calling; if the trace is successful (and not all are), a recording from the telephone company gives you further instructions. In areas where this is available, there's usually an installation charge and a charge for each time the option is used.

If you suspect your phone is being tapped, you can contact the phone company, but be aware that they can't always find taps that are actually there. To check for the possibility of phone taps or room bugs, it's best to contact a private investigator with strong experience in that particular area.

Your Own Credit History

The Fair Credit Reporting Act, which limits the instances when *other* people can investigate the contents of your credit file, also gives you permission to check that file at any time. To do this, contact one of the approximately 2,000 credit bureaus or consumer credit clearinghouses currently in existence. (Look in your local Yellow Pages under "Credit

Rating" or "Reporting" agencies or check with your local Better Business Bureau.)

Technically, these companies are only required to give you an oral or written credit history review, but in most instances they will furnish you with the same computer-generated compilation of facts that they give to companies that subscribe to their service (landlords, banks, retailers, etc.).

There is generally a fee for obtaining even your own credit history, except when you have been denied credit on the basis of a negative credit history. If that's the case, you usually have 30 days to obtain your report without a fee. Even if you haven't had any problem, it could be worthwhile to see what's in your report, especially if you suspect there may be an error or inaccuracy. You are entitled to question any item on your report that you believe to be inaccurate, misleading, or vague. The credit bureau is then required to investigate, and it must remove any item that can't be substantiated.

If the bureau confirms a damaging item, you still have the option of presenting a hundred-word explanation that must be placed in your file. Also be aware that any time an item is deleted or an explanation is added, you have the right to request that the credit bureau inform anyone who has received a report in the past six months.

Medical Records

As discussed earlier, medical records are not technically public records. But a hell of a lot of people have access to them, including insurance companies, employers, government agencies, and companies where you have applied for a job. If your current company self-insures, there's also a good chance that a variety of other employees have unlimited access to your medical records. Interestingly, there is no federal law that governs the confidentiality of personal medical records once they have been released from a doctor's office or hospital.

Many people are also not aware that their medical records may contain the personal opinion of the doctors they have consulted. Let's say you've gone to a doctor because you've been feeling tired and just not up to snuff lately. After recording this, the doctor may also note that you look sickly or seem depressed. While these notes may be important for his or her diagnosis, do you really want your employer to read that? There's also always a possibility that your doctor's interpretation is not in sync with what you believe or know to be true. Did you ever bother to go back to your internist and tell her that what she suspected was a psychiatric disorder was actually an allergy? Unless you want people reading about this presumed mental illness, maybe you should.

Also included in your medical records are the records of personal habits. Do you want your life insurance company to know that you generally smoke three packs of cigarettes a day or tend to drink a six-pack on Friday nights? If they have a copy of the standard form you filled out the first time you went to any doctor, they probably do know it. The point here is not whether or not you should do these things, rather that if you do choose to do them, it should be your right to decide who else knows about them.

Here are some other things that might show up on your records: the twice-weekly visits to your psychologist, the HIV test you take every six months, your prescription for insomnia or treatment for a sexually transmitted disease, the operation for your abortion or vasectomy, and so on.

Furthermore, your medical records can be subpoenaed in cases where they might be of aid to the opposition in some sort of lawsuit. For example, the lawyer for your soon-to-be-ex-spouse might want the medical records of the abortion you didn't tell your husband about, or the former employer you are suing might be interested in obtaining the records that detail your problem with alcohol. Needless to say, lawyers for the opposition will only be interested in records that help them with their side of a case.

While there is really no way to assure your complete medical privacy, here are some ways to cut down on the information that might be floating around about you:

1. Find out what your company's policy is on medical records. How many people at work have access to your medical records? Who receives the records? If you don't like the answers, let your company know.

2. If you do need to authorize the release of your medical records for any reason, don't sign a blanket release. Add a line stating that the release is only for a certain doctor for a certain condition. If not, the release can simply be copied and used again and again.

3. Make it clear to your doctor that your records are not to leave his or her office without your prior approval.

4. Find out the intent of any medical questionnaire that you fill out and feel free to refuse if not satisfied with the answer.

5. Obtain copies of your medical records if you have any doubts about the information contained in them. Many doctors will tell you that it is not their policy to let you have access to these records. Remind any doctor who takes this approach that they are *your* records. If that doesn't work, in 31 states, it's your *legal right* to obtain these records—a mention of that fact will change most doctors' minds. Contact your local American Medical Association to find out what the law is in your state.

6. The Medical Information Bureau (MIB) is a kind of

clearinghouse of medical information and records for approximately 750 insurance companies. Any company that subscribes to its services has access to every claim you've made over the past seven years. Approximately one in every seven Americans is on file with it. To see if it has a file on you and to ensure its accuracy, contact MIB at P. O. Box 105, Essex Station, Boston, Massachusetts 02112; (617) 426-3660.

7. If you want to ensure that there is no paper trail of certain treatments or tests that you undergo, pay for them in cash rather than going through your insurance company.

Other Personal Information

As computer capabilities increase, so does the number of ways that other people can keep track of you. It may sound like some bizarre vision of the future, but right now, just about anyone who wants to know anything about you can find out—if they have the time and the money.

Ever wonder how a company knows to send you coupons for headache medicines, but not your spouse? It's because they know that you buy headache remedies. How? Maybe you filled out a survey and said that you get frequent headaches. Maybe you used a coupon with your name and address on the back to purchase a headache medicine. Or maybe you are an accountant who subscribes to a trade magazine and the drug manufacturer reasoned that many accountants get headaches, so you probably do, too.

See if you have done any of the following in the past six months. If you have, you have probably unwittingly provided someone with a lot of information about yourself and your habits. They, in turn, can sell that information to anyone else who is interested.

- Have you subscribed to any magazines?
- Have you taken any classes?

- Have you taken any kind of free health test, such as a weight analysis or cholesterol screening?
- Have you called any 800 phone numbers? (Technology allows the recipient of the call to automatically capture your phone number; reverse phone books can then provide your name and address.)
- Have you ordered any products through the mail?
- Have you applied for any credit cards?
- Have you used any coupons that ask for your name, address, etc.?
- Have you entered any sweepstakes?
- Have you filled out any questionnaires or surveys?
- Have you donated money to any charitable organization or cause?

These are just *some* of the things that can put your name into a database or on a mailing list. To help cut down on the number of lists your name ends up on (as well as to eliminate some of your junk mail), you can write to the Direct Marketing Association and ask them to remove your name from mailing lists. It won't get you off all the lists but it will help. Their address is Mail Preference Service, Direct Marketing Association, P. O. Box 9008, Farmingdale, New York 11735-9008. With most credit cards, magazine subscriptions, etc., you can also write directly to the company requesting that your name not be sold to other mailing lists.

I'm not advising being paranoid—just aware. Know that anytime you give anyone information about yourself, you might be making that same information available to hundreds or thousands of other people.

14 | *So You Want To Be a Private Investigator*

OK, you've read this book and you're hooked. You want to be part of the fun, fascinating world of private investigators. First, a warning: You should have realized by now, it's not all fun and games.

Private investigators do a lot of work that's just downright boring. No, it's not fun to sit in a car parked in front of someone's house for twenty-four hours. Nor is it fun to search through hundreds of computer databases only to discover your subject has never done anything wrong. On the other hand, there is a real thrill when your subject finally does leave the house and you know you are finally onto something. Or when you obtain that critical piece of information that is going to save your client thousands of dollars or a major heartbreak.

Still interested? Your first piece of investigative work can be finding out what the rules governing private investigators are in your state. Here are the basics, but the rules vary from state to state.

In most states, private investigators must be licensed, although the licensing agency varies from state to state. It might be the state police, department of state, state consumer affairs bureau, or another agency. Usually three years of experience is required to obtain a license. The experience can generally be with a local, state, or federal government agency; or it can be gained working full-time for another private investigator. In some states the required experience is enough to get you the license; in others, there is an exam as well as an experience requirement.

In all states, you must have a clean record of your own. You'll usually have to fill out a lengthy application and provide substantial business and personal references. The whole process can take anywhere from three to six months, at the end of which time you receive your license. Along the way, you will also be required to have your fingerprints taken and in some states, you might be required to be bonded or insured.

Regardless of specific background, there are certain personality traits that private investigators tend to have. A natural curiosity and desire to uncover secrets is a requirement. Persistence is also essential—there will be times when it seems that nothing is ever going to come together or start making sense. A good investigator must be able to continue working through those times.

Those who do best at undercover work are people who can change and adapt themselves to any situation. It also helps to have a friendly, outgoing personality—the kind that encourages strangers to reveal confidences.

The best investigators, whether undercover or doing other kinds of searches, are those who know how to get information from people. These are the people who can mine gold from a casual chat at a bus stop, charm the iron-willed secretary into disclosing private information, entice an overworked bureaucrat to do just one small favor.

While there is certainly no minimum intelligence requirement for investigative work, a quick mind is a strong asset. You never know what kind of situation you're going to find yourself in. Investigators need to always be on the lookout, sometimes searching for information in the most unlikely places and circumstances. And, just as importantly, sometimes they need to be able to quickly get themselves *out* of dangerous situations.

Reading this book is a good start in terms of learning about what kind of information is available and how to obtain it. But your work isn't nearly done yet—now it's time to go out and practice! Good luck.

Appendix A: Social Security Numbers

If you know someone's Social Security number, you automatically know the state from which it was issued. Just look at the first three digits and compare them to the following state-by-state list. There's a good chance other public records concerning that person will be found in the same state.

001-003	New Hampshire	268-302	Ohio
004-007	Maine	303-317	Indiana
008-009	Vermont	318-361	Illinois
010-034	Massachusetts	362-386	Michigan
035-039	Rhode Island	387-399	Wisconsin
040-049	Connecticut	400-407	Kentucky
050-134	New York	408-415	Tennessee
135-158	New Jersey	416-424	Alabama
159-211	Pennsylvania	425-428	Mississippi
212-220	Maryland	429-432	Arkansas
221-222	Delaware	433-439	Louisiana
223-231	Virginia	440-448	Oklahoma
232-236	West Virginia	449-467	Texas
237-246	North Carolina	468-477	Minnesota
247-251	South Carolina	478-485	Iowa
252-260	Georgia	486-500	Missouri
261-267	Florida	501-502	North Dakota

503-504	South Dakota	531-539	Washington
505-508	Nebraska	540-544	Oregon
509-515	Kansas	545-573	California
516-517	Montana	574	Alaska
518-519	Idaho	575-576	Hawaii
520	Wyoming	577-579	District of
521-524	Colorado		Columbia
525, 585	New Mexico	580	Virgin Islands
526-527	Arizona	581-585	Puerto Rico, Guam,
528-529	Utah		American Samoa,
530	Nevada		Philippine Islands

Appendix B: Resources

Pamphlets

The following pamphlets are available for a fee from the Government Printing Office, Washington, D.C. 20402; (202) 512-0000.

- *Where to Write for Marriage Records*
- *Where to Write for Divorce Records*
- *Where to Write for Birth and Death Certificates*
- *The Information Book* contains the names, addresses, and phone numbers of every government office

Other helpful publications include:

- *How You May Save Time Proving Your Age and Other Birth Facts* from the U.S. Department of Health and Human Services, National Center for Health Statistics, Rockville, Maryland 20852
- *Genealogical Research in the National Archives*; National Archives Trust Fund Board, P. O. Box 100793, Atlanta, Georgia 30384

Specialized Libraries

- **The Family History Library of the Church of Latter Day Saints**, 35 Northwest Temple Street,

Salt Lake City, Utah, 84150; (801) 240-2331. The
most complete genealogical library in the world;
branch offices are located worldwide.
- **Kammandale Library**, 57 North Dale Street, St.
Paul, Minnesota 55102; (612) 224-5160. More than
35,000 books on topics related to any kind of
family search, such as adoptees and birth parents,
background, genealogical information, nationality,
and inheritance.

Information Suppliers

(For more information about any of the companies listed
here, see Chapter 6, "Using Information Brokers and Hiring
a Private Investigator.")

- **Easy Link**, 1 Lake Street, Upper Saddle River, New
Jersey 07458; (800) 435-7375.
- **CDB Infotek**, P. O. Box 5466, Orange, California
92613–5466; (800) 427-3747.
- **Information Resource Services Company (IRSC)**,
3777 N. Harbor Boulevard, Fullerton, California
92635; (800) 640-4772.
- **Prentice Hall**, 500 Central Avenue, Albany, New
York 12206; (800) 333-0431.
- **TRW Redi Property Data**, 1700 Northwest 66th
Avenue, Fort Lauderdale, Florida 33313; (800)
327-1072.
- **U.S. Datalink**, 6711 Bayway Drive, Baytown, Texas
77520; (800) 527-7930.

The Armed Forces

All branches of the armed forces now have computerized
locator services. See Chapter 7, "How to Find Anyone," for
more information on the offices listed below.

- **U.S. Army**, Worldwide Locator, U.S. Army Enlisted Records and Evaluation Center, Fort Benjamin Harrison, Indiana 46249–5301; (317) 542-4211.
- **U.S. Air Force**, Air Force Military Personnel Center, Worldwide Locator, Randolph AFB, Texas 78150; (512) 652-5775.
- **U.S. Navy**, Navy Locator Service, Navy Annex Building, Washington, D.C. 20370; (703) 614-3155.
- **U.S. Marine Corps**, USMC CMC, HQMC MM5B-10, 2008 Elliot Road, Suite 201, Quantico, Virginia 22134–5030; (703) 640–3942.
- **U.S. Coast Guard**, Commander MPC-s, Military Personnel Command, 2100 2nd Street, S.W., Washington, D.C. 20593–0001; (202) 267–1340.
- **Retired Military and Civil Service Personnel**, The Office of Personnel Management, 1900 E. Street, S.W., Washington, D.C. 20415.

Adoption Information Organizations

The following are national organizations and resources that can help with your search. See Chapter 8, "Adoptee/ Birth Parent Searches" for more information about each organization.

- **Adoptees Liberty Movement Association (ALMA)**, P. O. Box 727, Radio City Station, New York, New York 10101-0727; (212) 581-1568.
- **Adoption Search Institute**, P. O. Box 11749, Costa Mesa, California 92627.
- **American Adoption Congress**, 1000 Connecticut Avenue, N.W., Suite 9, Washington, D.C. 20036.
- **International Soundex Reunion Registry**, P. O. Box 2312, Carson City, Nevada 89702.

Additional Information Sources

Your search for public records and information may take
you to a variety of sources. Here are some of the more
common offices that you might want to contact:

- **Bureau of the Census**, Pittsburg, Kansas 66762
- **Federal Aviation Administration (FAA)**, Regional
  Offices. For information regarding aircraft and pilot
  licensing.
- **Immigration and Naturalization Service**, 119 D
  Street, N.W., Washington, D.C. 20536, (202)
  514-2000.
- **Mail Preference Service**, Direct Marketing
  Association, P. O. Box 9008, Farmingdale, New York
  11735-9008. To have your name removed from
  mailing lists.
- **The Medical Information Bureau (MIB)**, P. O. Box
  105, Essex Station, Boston, Massachusetts 02112;
  (617) 426-3660. A kind of clearinghouse of medical
  information and records for approximately 750
  insurance companies.
- **National Archives and Records Administration**,
  Pennsylvania Avenue, N.W., Washington, D.C.
  20408; call (202) 501-5402.
- **National Center for Missing and Exploited
  Children**, 2101 Wilson Boulevard, Suite 550,
  Arlington, Virginia 22201–3052; (800) 843-5678,
  (703) 235-3900. A nonprofit clearinghouse that
  collects, compiles, disseminates, and exchanges
  information on missing children.
- **National Drivers Registration Service**, U.S.
  Department of Commerce, 1717 H Street,
  Washington, D.C. 20510. Agency established to
  help law enforcement officials and insurance
  companies trace people who have a suspended or

revoked license in one state and who apply for a license in another state.

- **National Runaway Hotline**, (800) 621-4000.
- **Passport Services**, Correspondence Branch, U.S. Department of State, Washington, D.C. 20524.
- **Secretary of Defense**, Washington, D.C. 20301. For information regarding deaths of anyone in the Army, Navy, Marines, or Air Force.
- **U.S. Coast Guard**, Commandant, P. S., Washington, D.C. 20226. For information regarding deaths while a member of the Coast Guard.
- **U.S. Social Security Administration**, OCRO, Division of Certification and Coverage, 300 North Greene Street, Baltimore, Maryland 21201.

| *Index*